WISCONSIN
My Home

WISCONSIN

MY HOME

The story of Thurine Oleson
as told to her daughter
ERNA OLESON XAN

THE UNIVERSITY OF WISCONSIN PRESS

Published 1950
The University of Wisconsin Press
Box 1379, Madison, Wisconsin 53701

The University of Wisconsin Press, Ltd.
1 Gower Street, London WC1E 6HA, England

Printings 1950, 1952, 1975, 1978

Printed in the United States of America
ISBN 0-299-00711-1 cloth, 0-299-00714-6 paper
LC 51-373

Dedicated to

The Oleson Children

With all the love of our hearts

CONTENTS

ACKNOWLEDGMENTS

IN PREPARING this book, the authors are greatly indebted to various members of the family for their generous help with stories, pictures, and family lists. The genealogy was a winter's work, and could not have been gathered together without the cheerful assistance of all the "sisters and the cousins and the aunts."

The authors realize that there may be mistakes in the genealogy, although every name has been checked and double-checked by several people. In all cases we tried to contact the oldest members of the particular branch. Where families have moved to distant places and have not kept in touch with those back home, it was difficult to make the list complete. For this, we apologize. We hope the name-spellings are right. If there are mistakes, they were not intended.

We wish to thank in particular for their kind and painstaking assistance John M. and Isabel Olson and their daughter-in-law, Mabel; Sarah Uvaas and her daughters, Lillian and Myrtle; Clara Lindgren, Ole and Stella Thompson, Mable and Irene Johnson, and Ida Ziem; Henry and Lena Larsen, Julia Olson, Thone Olson and her daughter, Tillie Bockmann; Chris Thompson, Arthur and Hilda Larsen, Charlotte and Ellis Johnson, John Böe of Butte des Morts, Barney Barstow, Evelyn Baxandall, Herman Olson; and Cora and Harvey Peterson who went out in the dead of winter and read inscriptions on tombstones in Winneconne. We wish to thank especially Cousin Olav Böe, Administrative Director of "Norske Folk" of Oslo, for the names of the descendants of Stor Ole Böe. Without the help of these people and many others, we would have been greatly handicapped.

We also wish to thank Miss Mary Lou Warrick of Madison, Wisconsin, for the sketches used on the title and half-title pages.

And to John and Dixie Xan we express our deepest appreciation for their steadfast encouragement and support in all phases of the work.

THE AUTHORS

NORWAY

ONE OF MY earliest memories is of Mother rocking by the window in the old log house, smoking her clay pipe and crying about Norway. In the deep window sill near by was the polished maple tobacco box with brass hinges, which she had brought with her across the sea. In opposite chairs were Old Country cronies, Bergit Lund or Signe Maurubrekke. Three-cornered scarves covered their smooth greying hair, swept down over their wrinkled cheeks, to tie neatly in a knot under their busy chins. Their full skirts touched the floor at each forward dip of the rockers.

All the afternoon they sat and cried and rocked. "Have you heard from your brother in Sauland? . . . Do you remember the time we used to go up to the mountain pastures? . . . Wouldn't you like to taste again the red *multer* berries that grew in the woods?" Now it would be talk of the snow that was lying on the graves of their loved ones by the old *stavkirke*. Now they would sigh over the lavender silk-flowers and red lilies blooming about the mountain meadows. By and by the clock would strike four. Mother, reaching into the seam-pocket of her skirt, would pull out her handkerchief, wipe the tears, and go to the stove to make coffee.

All of our people came from Telemarken, Norway. Dozens and dozens of them had emigrated to the Town of Winchester in east central Wisconsin. I was the first child born of my parents in the New World. What I shall tell you of the Old Country are the stories I heard when these old friends got together, and when, after supper night after night, Father and Mother talked of Norway and nothing else.

Mother and Father were married about 1847. She was twenty-two years old then, and he thirty-five. They were probably married in a *stavkirke*, one of those small, richly-carved wooden churches, centuries old. In Hitterdal, Father's birthplace, was one of the most beautiful of them, on the Kongsberg-Telemark road. These churches had high-pitched, wooden shingle roofs, rising in tiers like the sides of a pyramid. My folks, however, were married in Sauland *Kirke*, near Mother's home. Mother was Thorild Böe, youngest child of a well-to-do family. They owned Gaarden Böe, that is, the Böe farm. It was a fairly big farm, and the family was one of the finest in this Sauland (Sheepland) church. They had the best horses and two-wheeled carts in summer, and the finest *spirs* (sleighs) for winter. This seemed to mean a lot to them and make them important, as an expensive automobile does now. At least, we heard often from Mother about their carts and horses and sleighs. Sometimes the women rode horseback to church, with the men walking alongside. They said that when Mother was young she rode a white horse like the wind, with a flock of young men galloping after.

Father was thirteen years older than Mother. He also came from respectable Christian people, and they were quite wealthy for that country. Three of his brothers were schoolmasters, which was something unusual. Great stress was laid on Family and Money in Norway—altogether too much. People would often marry cousins to keep the farm in the family. I am happy to tell you, however, that my parents were not related, and that it was a real love match which lasted fifty-eight years.

I have often been told by those who saw her, that Mother was the most beautiful bride that ever entered Sauland *Kirke*. She was of medium height, with strong limbs, serious grey eyes, and heavy black hair. Her skin was rose and white, and she was superbly healthy. On this great day she wore the guimpe which her mother, Signe, had made for her own wedding in 1810. It was of hand-woven linen with long, full sleeves and a stiff, high, stand-up collar. This collar was a solid mass of tiny stitches in intricate and many-colored designs, made by counting the threads. Down the sides of the neck opening was a swirl of colored silk embroidery, closed at the top by a silver circle with a sharp prong at the back. With this guimpe went some sort of bodice and a long billowing skirt, held at the waist by a hand-woven ceremonial sash in blue and green and yellow, which had been worn by six generations of Böe women. A headdress of thin silver flowers and leaves rested on the thick black hair which flowed down her back.

Father's wedding outfit consisted of woolen knee breeches with six silver buttons down each side. There were silver buttons on his coat. His shoulder-length hair was black and as fine as silk, and his wide felt hat was turned up all around. The long stockings he wore

4

were knit of real fine yarn in blue and white, and held up with leather garters buckled in silver. Father was about six feet tall, with gentle eyes of dark blue and face clean shaven. Nothing ever seemed to ruffle Father. He was always calm, but his eyes would twinkle when there was a good joke. It was said that Mother was so popular and high-spirited as a girl that she was always in the middle of a chattering ring. She was the quicker thinker of the two, and always made the decisions in our house.

There was one person at the wedding that I must mention. This was a slender child about eleven years old, with lively blue eyes that took in everything. Her name was Tone Daalaan. Her folks and Mother's folks were acquainted, belonging to the same church, but the difference in social station kept them apart. Tone heard that there was going to be a great wedding in the church and determined to go. She did not see much grandeur in her life. Although her folks were poor, they were honorable and respectable, and good Christians. To lack these qualities in Telemarken, you were a nobody. So little Tone slipped into the church uninvited and watched the wedding. She was the one that told me of the beautiful bride with silver headdress over the long black hair, and the richly embroidered clothing. When it was over, she watched the sleek fat horses prancing up to take the guests home for the wedding feast. Little Tone did not dream on that day that all of them would be transported to America, and that she would be rich, and they poor. And she certainly never imagined that her only son, John, would marry a daughter of that wealthy couple. That was my husband, and me.

My folks were married by Pastor Finkenhagen. A regular Jewish name, but he was Norwegian to the backbone. This same man had confirmed my mother in the Lutheran faith, and he later baptized several of her children. Now he went, of course, with all the relatives and friends to the wedding feast at Gaarden Böe, leaving little Tone to trudge home alone. There Mother Signe tossed off her wedding shawl and bonnet and hustled the servants to bring out the wedding ale she had made so carefully. They must bring on the fancy cakes and cookies, and the special white breads made weeks beforehand. Great platters of roasted meats were borne to

5

the long tables. The painted, hand-carved wooden goblets were filled again and again. The steaming coffee poured rich and golden into the waiting cups, pitchers of thick cream and bowls of sugar lumps bought in the city for such occasions were urged upon the guests. Cheeses of infinite variety, white and yellow, and green and gold, mounds of yellow butter, and bowls of creamy potatoes were passed from hand to hand. The servants came in with bottles of homemade strawberry wine, whereby all the guests might toast the blushing bride sitting at the seat of honor with her timid, adoring Mathis.

When all had eaten and drunk to a state of merriment, the tables were cleared away and the fiddlers called in. How they could put the rhythm and fire into the feet! How the full skirts twirled as the hands linked above the heads in the wonderful wedding dances! Stout shoes stomped on the thick sturdy, board floor, manly arms circled delicate waists and a brief vow of love would be whispered in a waiting ear before they parted in another measure. Darkness fell and still they danced. Supper was called, then again the skirling of a fresh set of fiddlers would set them going anew. This went on for days, until everybody, including the bride and groom, was exhausted.

When the last guest had finally departed, the bridal couple packed up their goods and went to a farm that Father had bought near by. It was called the Leine farm. Father then dropped his old childhood farm name of Haevre, as was the custom in Norway. He was afterwards known as Mathis Olson Leine. A few years later, they moved farther away to the Juve farm, and then he had to change his name to Juve and drop the Leine. This Juve farm was in Gvamen, near Skeie, in Hjartdal, so an old cousin told me.

The Juve farm was hilly, and there were woods on it. On one side of the farm buildings was a big hill, but the other side was good flat land. House and *stabbur* (food building) were both of logs. Once a friend came there drunk. For a joke he led a horse to the upstairs of the *stabbur*, but the steps were so solid that they did not break under the weight. He was too drunk to get the horse back down the steps, and the men of the family had to come to its rescue and back it down. The cow stable was on level ground, and between it and the house was space for visitors' horses and carriages. Above the cow stable were bunks for the *budeie* (chore girls), who took care of the cows. Only one servant stayed in the house; her name was Big Helga.

The log house on this farm had two stories: the downstairs with kitchen, beds, and bunks, and the *opstue*, a kind of upstairs living room used for company, of which they had a great deal. It was from this custom of taking the company to the *opstue* that the men, even when they settled in America, went upstairs to play cards and smoke and talk when we had a crowd.

The kitchen on the Juve farm was dominated by a big fireplace in which they burned the abundant logs from their land. Father was faithful at keeping Mother supplied with wood. The fireplace had a long crane to hang kettles on. Mother was very fond of her kitchen utensils and took many of them with her to America. I remember two copper teakettles, a small one to make coffee in, and a bigger one for heating water. She also brought with her a huge copper kettle the size of a small wash tub, with a strong bale, in which she cooked her *prim* (whey cheese). Even in this country, this kettle had to stand over an outdoor fire whenever she made *prim*. This fire was in a stone fireplace that Father made, like the one he had in Norway.

Silver was plentiful in the Old Country, not only for buttons and buckles and headdresses but also for silver spoons for the table. For everyday they used wooden spoons with short, carved handles and bowls about like a tablespoon. Father was a fine wood carver. I suppose these wooden spoons were not as cold to the lips in winter as the silver. A good many of the bowls in which food was served were carved out of wood, as well as the goblets and kitchen utensils.

I heard plenty about the delicious food in Norway. One of their favorite dishes was clabbered milk with the cream left on it. Another was egg pancakes. I was always amused to hear them refer to egg yolks as "egg plums." They ate a lot more meat in Norway than in America—beef, mutton, and pork. In the spring it would be lamb and veal. Some salted meats would last the year 'round. Fish was always on hand—herring, trout, and *lutefisk*. Mother said she was good at catching speckled trout in the mountain streams.

The men did fishing with nets. They often broiled their catch over the coals in the kitchen fireplace.

But the main dish was a pudding called *gröt* (pronounced "grout"). It was usually eaten for supper. A common variety was made with milk and flour, salted to taste and called *velling*. Another popular kind was *potetgröt*. Mother made it this way: First she cooked potatoes until they were falling to pieces, then mashed them in the water they were cooked in. Into this she sifted flour and stirred until it was thick, seasoning it with the coarse cooking salt from the jar by the fireplace. The flour would lump a little, of course, and she would stir it vigorously with a *grötturu* that Father had made for her. She was not satisfied until the *gröt* was white and smooth, and never liked to feel little uncooked lumps of dough in her mouth.

Now it was ready to dip up on plates, with a generous lump of butter in a hollow of the steaming pudding, whose sides would presently be trickling with yellow streams. Each place would be set with a plate of this, a spoon and a cup of milk. How happy the family was to sit down to the good meal, say the blessing, and go to eating. To eat *gröt*, one first dipped a spoonful of it into the melted butter, then into the cup of milk, then into the hungry waiting mouth it went. No one ever tired of it.

Risgryngröt was made of rice, flour, milk, water, and salt cooked together until real soft, stirred all the time with the *grötturu*. At table, sugar and cinnamon were sprinkled over this before dipping into the milk. They did not have this kind as often, because rice had to be bought in town.

If there was special company, or if it was Christmas or Easter, and surely whenever there was a new baby, then *römmegröt* was made out of pure cream (*römme*). Mother thought nothing of using a quart of cream for this delicious dish. She poured it into a round bottom iron kettle and put it over the fire. When it began to boil, she began to sift in flour, and salt to taste, and stirred it until the cream rose to the top. It had to be stirred with the *grötturu* every moment to keep from lumping and sticking to the bottom of the kettle.

Now, this *grötturu* was made from a certain peeled and polished

8

pine limb, with a ring of five up-shooting small branches at the end. Father had cut the branches to about three inches long before he peeled and polished it. The handle was about fifteen inches long. Big Helga or one of the older girls had to stand beside Mother, who was sifting the flour into the cream, and twirl the handle of this primitive egg beater between their palms, while the five prongs kept the *gröt* in swirls and waves every minute. When the *gröt* became thick, milk was added to the right amount, and if the cream had not risen properly, as much butter as needed was added to make it richer. This, too, was served hot on plates. It was often sprinkled with sugar and cinnamon before dipping into the melted butter and milk.

If Mother was going to give this as a gift, she would carry as much as a two-quart panful to the new mother. The top would be stuck full of sugar lumps or sprinkled with sugar and cinnamon. Then she would say, "I have brought you some *gröt* to make you strong." In winter, this pudding would keep until it was used up, and the new mother served some of it each day. She was supposed to drink a lot of homemade beer, too, to make milk. When my mother had babies in Norway, she had such excellent care and diet that by the time she got out of bed, there would be a dimple on top of every knuckle on her hands. The babies in Norway were so fat from rich mother's milk, and the mild *römmegröt* fed them later, that they were like balls of butter, and seldom sick. Babies did not have special beds in Norway, but were bundled up and put to sleep above the mother's head on the pillow.

There was a trained woman who went around in the fall to bake the winter's supply of *flatbröd* (flatbread). This was a sort of crisp, cracker-like bread baked in round sheets, which they ate daily, since yeast bread was used only for Christmas and Easter. First they took a quart of flour, a cup of cornmeal, and a cup of whole wheat flour, and sifted it with salt to taste. They then scalded it with boiling water and mixed it into a dough, adding four table-spoons of butter in the process. Now this mass was allowed to cool while Mother prepared the table for rolling out, for it needed lots of room. The long thin rolling pin she used for this purpose was carved by Father, and was grooved in spirals to spread the dough

9

better. When the dough was cool enough to handle, she sprinkled flour on her mixing board on the table and began to work a ball of the dough into an even round shape as big as a milk pan, maybe seventeen inches across. In the meantime the *flatbröd* woman was busy scouring off the stove top or griddle on which these sheets were to be baked. She had to make it shine, for Mother wanted no little black burned specks through her bread. In America *flatbröd* was baked right on the lids of the wood cook stove.

The secret of making *flatbröd* was to roll the sheets so thin that they barely hung together. To lift this big thin sheet off the table and onto the stove and not break it, Mother used a long wooden spatula called a *brödskoru*. She started at one side of the sheet and rolled the *flatbröd* gently over the spatula, then unrolled it carefully onto the hot griddle. Just as much skill was needed to turn it when it was browned on one side. Mother slipped the spatula under it, and with her hand steadied it till it was flipped over on the other side to brown. When it was baked, it was lifted back onto the table to cool. After this, the sheets were stacked like round cardboards and stored in a cool, clean place. *Flatbröd* kept all winter and was eaten at will. It was always as crisp as a fresh soda cracker. To eat it, one broke off a small piece and buttered it. We often ate it unbuttered, broken up in a bowl of milk.

Another popular bread was *lefse*, but it could not be stored like *flatbröd*. It had a potato base. To make *lefse*, Mother took twenty boiled Irish potatoes, mashed them fine and added two tablespoons of melted butter or a half-cup of cream, and salt to taste. Then she added enough flour to permit rolling out. If it became too dry, she added a half cup of potato water. The ball of *lefse* dough that was pinched off would make the size of a dinner plate when rolled out. She used a smooth rolling pin·for this. The dough had to be very thin and was baked on the griddle or top of stove. When it was slightly brown, Mother turned it over with the *brödskuru* and baked it on the other side. *Lefse* was not crisp like *flatbröd*, but limp and soft like a pancake. It was folded over when taken off the stove. Norwegians liked *lefse* hot or cold, and buttered. Some rolled it up like a pancake and ate it out of hand. Pickled pigs' feet or *lutefisk* were a favorite accompaniment.

This *lutefisk* was a much prized dish in Norway. It was made from a fish called *torsk* caught in the ocean in summer. It was cleaned and cut in halves lengthwise and laid on stones to dry in the sun for about three or four weeks, until the halves became very hard. Boatloads of this dried fish were shipped to other countries. The housewife had to know a long time ahead when she wanted to serve *lutefisk*, because it had to be soaked in water for two weeks. Even then, *lutefisk* was not a dish one could make up her mind to prepare between dinner and supper, because now it had to be soaked again in lye water that was made from the ashes of peeled maple wood. It must stand in this lye water until the fish was soft enough to allow the fingers to touch through the meat when pinched.

Yet the meat was not ready to cook. It must be soaked again in clear water overnight. The next day it was skinned and cut into serving pieces. Then one must place it in a cloth and drop it into boiling salted water and boil it until the meat was firm, three to five minutes. *Lutefisk* went to the table on a platter, strewn with melted butter, or a rich milk gravy with a lot of butter in it. It was served with mashed potatoes and *lefse*.

Christmas was celebrated for three weeks in Norway. Therefore, a good deal of butchering and baking had to be done beforehand. Stacks of *flatbröd* had been put aside, and now it was time to make the cookies called *kringler* and *fattigmand*. *Kringler* were made in the shape of a ring. For this, Mother creamed together a cup of butter and a cup of sugar and added two eggs, beaten till very light. To this she added a half cup of milk and one teaspoon of caraway seed. Enough flour was added to make a dough stiffer than cake batter, but not as stiff as regular cookie dough. She then pinched off a small piece, rolled it under her hands to about six or eight inches long, deftly tied it into a bowknot, and baked it on a pan in a hot oven. These simply melted in one's mouth.

The name *"fattigmand"* (poor man) is a joke, for it is a very rich cookie. Cream was the fat in this, three tablespoons of it, mixed with three tablespoons of sugar. To this was added three eggs and the whole beaten for fifteen minutes with a wooden spoon until it was light yellow and fluffy. One teaspoon each of cardamon seed and of brandy were added. Now enough flour was sifted and folded in to make a stiff dough. A plain rolling pin was used to roll it very thin. It was cut in squares or oblongs with a knife, and each square pricked with the knife-point. When *fattigmand* was baked in hot grease in a skillet, the square corners all turned up. After they were slightly browned, they were lifted out of the skillet and laid on a board to cool. *Fattigmand* had to be stored in boxes in another room, out of temptation, to await the feasting time. Christmas was a great season for visiting and company, and Mother was always amply prepared. She taught all her daughters to make these good Norwegian dishes.

You can see by these foods that they knew how to live well. They had to eat well to keep up strength for the active life they led. There were no idle people in Norway, although they did not drive themselves as we do here. Everybody had something to do at all times. If a man had nothing to do, he carved spoons and goblets. If a woman found time on her hands, she picked up her knitting. Even the children were kept busy. The women made cloth at home. Mother had a spinning wheel and a loom, on which all the cloth for the household was woven. She brought her spinning wheel with her to America, in pieces in a chest. It was light blue trimmed with a yellow stripe around the wheel. Yellow and white decorations were painted here and there. My folks raised their own sheep for wool, even in this country. Mother spun all the wool needed for mittens and stockings until she was seventy years old. In the early days in America, she even spun wool for blankets, underwear, and shirts for the men. In Norway they had flax for their lighter clothing and towels.

This sounds as if Mother had a lot of work to do, but even with her seven children in Norway, she never strained herself. Being the baby of the family at the Böe farm, she had never been made to do much work. Housework wasn't a great item in Norway, any-way. The floors were mopped only at Christmas and Easter. The rest of the time they were swept with homemade brooms until they shone. Mother was so clean, though, that she was always sweeping the floors, even as a girl. One day her mother said, "Don't spend so much time sweeping, dear. You can't make a living with the broom."

From her girlhood, Mother was used to having plenty of servants. There were three houses for the *husmenn* at the Böe farm. These were poor people who were glad to get their living quarters free, and a little pay, for the help they gave about the place. The Böes always kept women servants in the house.

Mother and Father had only one *husmann* at the Juve farm, and only one servant girl for the house. She was Big Helga. It was Helga who took charge of the children and carried the switch under her apron. If there was too much work for Helga, then someone was sent for the *husmann's* wife. The *husmann* himself helped Father whenever he was needed on the farm. When there was no work at our place, these people hired out elsewhere, and thus earned their living. Mother was so tenderhearted that she could never work these homeless people very hard. She never wanted to work very hard herself. Big Helga stayed with Mother for thirteen years, and Mother never forgot her. Signe Maurubrekke, who smoked a pipe with Mother in America, was one of the servants from Gaarden Böe. You can believe that Mother and she had good times talking about the old days.

Besides the housework, the women in Norway took care of the livestock; that is, Mother was in charge, but the chore girls did the work. This was because the men worked in the woods in winter, cutting timber to sell. In summer when the men tended the crops, the women had to take the cattle and sheep to the *seter* (mountain pasture) where the grass was lush and green.

It was just after St. Hans's Day (June 24) that they went up there. Each farmer owned or rented a log cabin up in the mountains and used it for two months every summer. Two *bönder* (farmers) and a girl from each farm often occupied the same *seter*. Father owned his own *seter*. You had to climb a mountain to get there, then there was a lovely green valley where the *seter* buildings were. Two girls had to watch the cows all day. Nearly every cow wore a bell, and all the ringing together made such a beautiful sound in the clear mountain air. There was a certain man who made the bells. Norwegians were so fond of bells that they even put them on horses in winter, big ones the size of a man's fist, two on each hame on top of the horse collar. They were called *dom bjeller* and were etched in fancy designs. When the horses trotted, the bells made a pretty sound.

There was a man named Andres Uvaas who went to America, and later came back to Norway for a visit. He had become so lonesome for these Norwegian bells that he determined to take some back with him. But it was against ship's regulations to have bells in the luggage. Andres filled them with flour in his trunk so that they could not ring, and in this manner he brought them through. My brother John still has two of those bells, and they have a clear, sweet, musical sound, as if there .were silver mixed in the metal.

In our family it was Mother who went to the *seter* with the herd. She loved to tend the cows and make butter and cheese. Besides, it was a delightful change from routine, like going to a wonderful mountain resort where the air was fresh and the sky vast and blue. She would take at least one of the older children to help look after the cattle, as well as one of the chore girls, and of course, the baby would have to be with her. Little brother John used to love to go because he got all the sweet cream he could eat up there. The home and the other children were left in the care of Father and Big Helga. Father would visit up on the mountain often, to get up wood and do anything else that he could, but Mother never left her post all summer.

Once when Father was walking up in the mountains, he found a small axe with two up-curved ends. The two bent prongs at the top must have fitted into holes in a handle, he thought. But the handle had long since rotted away. Father scoured off the blade to find out what it could have been. He saw on its side the imprint of the midnight sun, and as he carried it home, he pondered on its origin. Nothing like it had he ever seen before. After a while he came to the conclusion that it was a Viking battle-axe. Ever practical, he took the axe to his workshop and fitted across the top a stout handle of wood. Bringing it with a pleased look to his wife, he said: "Thorild, here is a chopping-knife for you. I know you will make me lots of good things to eat with it."

"Mathis, Mathis!" she replied with a tender smile. "That I surely will." And she used it all the rest of her life. It still has the sharpest edge of any chopping-knife I ever saw.

14

Mother was an excellent cheese-maker, and a clean one; always a great one to use lots of water. She got her supply from some mountain stream up there at the *seter*. The milk pails were made of wood, and the butter and cheese were kept in small wooden tubs. Just as there was a special person to make *flatbröd*, so there was a certain man who went around making tubs and pails, although Father was very handy at it himself. If you were not careful with wooden receptacles, things kept in them would taste rancid. But not under Mother's hand. She would scour them with sand, and wash them, scald them in boiling water, rinse in cold water, and then set them in the sun to sweeten and dry. I believe it was the great care given to the utensils, and the fresh cool air, that enabled them to keep their supplies fresh and sweet all the year 'round.

While Mother was gone up to the *seter*, great activity was taking place at home. Father and the older children, and the *husmann*, were busy tilling the soil of the small scattered fields. The farms were not large in Norway, only about forty or fifty acres, and not all of that was tillable land. But it must have been very fertile, and the people exceptional farmers, for they lived bountifully, both man and beast. In those short summer months they raised enough not only to keep a big family going all winter but to support six or eight cows, a couple of horses, and flocks of sheep and chickens.

The hay was cut and raked by hand, and that was slow work. Grain was cut by sickle. It was an older girl's job to cut and bind the straw into bundles. The main crops raised were barley, wheat, oats, and potatoes. The barley was ground into flour and used for mush, or for malt to make the *juleöl* (Christmas ale). The oats were fed to the stock, and some of the crop was used to make *flatbröd*. Some of the wheat was ground whole for baking, some made into white flour for the Christmas and Easter celebrations. Those were the only times that white flour was used extensively. On the Christmas loaves of white yeast bread, Mother would lay a twisted piece of dough in the form of an X.

They raised garden stuff, too, in summer. Carrots and cabbages could be stored in the cellar with the potatoes for the daily soups, whose base was meat seasoned with thyme; these were their winter fare. In summer they raised lettuce. They also picked the abundant wild berries—raspberries, strawberries, blueberries, and the delicious red *multer*. These grew low on bushes, making a red carpet in the woods. There was never any attempt to preserve fruits for winter use.

In the latter part of August, when it began to get cold, Father would go with horses and wagon up to the *seter* to bring Mother home. Most horses in Norway were not very big, and those Father owned were buckskin in color. For this shade they were named Skimmerton and Blakken. The wagon would have to be left down on the road, of course, but the horses would be loaded with butter, *gammelost* (old cheese) and *prim* that Mother had made, and then the great procession started. Pack horses led by Father, Mother carrying the baby, chore girls and children driving the herd, calves gamboling alongside and bells ringing—it must have been quite a sight and sound. Down at the road everything that could be was packed into the wagon, and Father helped Mother and the baby up into the seat for the journey home. From there they looked with eager eyes for the roof tops of the Juve place. You can imagine how glad Mother was to see the older children again as they came running to meet her, for our family always held deep affection for each other and enjoyed the mutual company. Big Helga would come bustling out with a wide smile on her face, announcing that she had a hot meal ready and that she hoped the mistress would find everything to her liking. Father and the older children and servants had to hustle the food into the *stabbur*, hardly able to wait for the supper. This *stabbur* was the most important building on the place, because all the food was stored there—grain, meat, and dairy products. The potatoes that had been grown on the farm lowlands would have to be stored in the cellar under the living-house to keep them from freezing.

Down there on the farm, the water for the house and barn was drawn up in buckets from a well, which had a little house built around it. But there were no pumps in Norway. The little washing that was done in winter was done with melted snow. In summer they took the clothes to a river and spanked them clean with a paddle on a stone.

Bedsheets were not used in Norway. Sheep pelts were used to sleep on in winter, and thin blankets in summer. These pelts would still have the wool on them, the hides tanned as soft as the softest blanket. When enough of these hides had been collected, another trained person was called in to make them into a big blanket. This tailor came in the fall of the year. In addition to the sheep blankets, he made the winter clothing out of heavy wool cloth that the women had woven. He would sew all day, but when it was getting dusk, and he couldn't see very well any more, he would lie down and take a nap until the evening meal was ready. Even in America I can remember that Mother would call dusk "the tailor's hour."

THE PEOPLE in Norway were so strong that they thought nothing of walking a couple of Norwegian miles, which were as long as seven of ours over here. One time Mother got homesick for Gaarden Böe, probably one Norwegian mile away. Taking her youngest baby, she left the house in charge of Big Helga and started out to walk. It must have been either in the early spring or fall, before or after *seter* time. She never forgot this beautiful walking journey, with great pine trees swaying up over her head, filling the air with spicy fragrance. Elm and oak trees cast shadows across her path at times. The streams in Norway were swift and clear, and there were waterfalls everywhere. She often told us of the *Rjukanfos* (Rjukan Falls) which were 415 feet high.

There was little to be afraid of alone in the woods, scarcely nothing more than the mourning doves whose plaintive calls echoed through the trees. The wolves in that country seemed to have died off from some disease. Bears had taken to the highlands, and Mother saw them only when she was up on the *seter*, and then not often. There were plenty of foxes, of course, slinking along their way to some farmer's chicken yard. To be sure, there were *orms* (snakes), both coppersnakes and blacksnakes. Of these she had not only a natural, but a Biblical fear. She also had to look out that she did not step on lizards that would dart into her path. Every now and then a hare would bound down the road ahead of her, and she would think of the pitiful little song about him:

What harm have I done to the people
That they should lay a snare in the way for me?

There never was a tramp that would harm or kill a wayfarer that we ever heard of. If there had been such a danger, Father would never have let her go on such a trip alone, and on foot. There seemed to be only two bad men about at that time. One was Ole Höiland (Highland), and the other Gjest Baardson. They were two noted thieves, who would rob houses, stores, and banks. Ole Höiland tried to justify himself by giving some of his loot to the poor. One time these two thieves met in the night, and did not recognize each other. Thinking the other a pursuer, each took off in the opposite direction as fast as he could. Later on, so the story went, they found out the joke on themselves. Finally Gjest was caught and put in prison, where he had to stay a long time. I can always remember the sad song he dictated to his sweetheart, whom he never expected to see again. It began like this:

If ever you hear this song
Think of one who loves but thee
And wish that I'll get free.

Without mishap, Mother reached her old home and had a comforting visit and a good rest. When she started back, her aging father walked with her quite a way in the woods. When he finally came to the place where he had to turn back, he could not bear to see her go off alone. She remembered all her life with tears how he called tenderly, "Do you want me to take you a little farther, *Mor* (Little Mother)?"

She called back, "No, Father, I shall be all right." And went the rest of the way home sadly. It was one of the last glimpses she ever had of him.

We did not hear so much about Father's people, for he was a quiet man and did not have much to say. I remember, though, that they told me about one time when he and his oldest son, Ole, went to an auction held at his brother's place. This man was one of the three schoolmasters I mentioned. He had married a very wealthy widow who was thrifty to a fault. They had no children. When he died, she would not give one of his personal things away, but sent out announcements of this auction. All of Father's people thought that they ought to have some little share in the estate, because brother had left no heirs to share the money and personal property he had left. But the lawyer told them it was no use even to try. He said that the widow had so much money of her own that she would win the case.

This brother had been a schoolmaster for years. Upon his retirement, he went around preaching and holding revival meetings. There was no end to all the books he had. Brother Ole, who was then only ten or twelve years old, wanted a certain New Testament he had taken a fancy to. Everybody laughed when this youngster piped up an offer of a half-dollar. But the auctioneer, instead of asking for more bids, called out: "Let the boy have the book!" And he got it. This book has quite large print and measures about four by eight inches. The binding is genuine leather, tooled in a pretty design. Ole read this book every day of his life, even to the age of ninety-five. He lived with me a couple of years in his old age, and I took care of him during his last illness. So the book came to me.

Now INTO this peaceful Norway, where there was plenty and to spare, a wind came creeping, slowly, stealthily. It chilled the old folks to the marrow, but it set the blood of the young on fire, their ears to tingling. Their eyes lit with a wild desire. For this wind whispered, "America . . . America . . . the Land of Gold . . . the New Land. . . ." Elders fought against it, they argued, they pleaded. But the wind blew only the stronger, sweeping them toward the sea with a mighty force. "America . . . America!"

Among the first of our family to go was Mother's older sister, Anne Böe, and her husband, Torger Olsson Landsverk. He was my husband's grandfather's brother. This was in the early 1840's. They settled first at Muskego in southern Wisconsin, and were charter members of the Norwegian Lutheran church there in 1846. They did their trading in Milwaukee, which then had only two stores. The proprietor of the one they patronized was a most hospitable man. He would never let them drive back to their farm until they had come up to his apartment above the store and had coffee and lunch.

In 1847 they made their way up to the Town of Winchester, where other Norwegians had found rich level land. It is said that the reason immigrants did not like southern Wisconsin in those days was that there were so many rattlesnakes. When they cut their grain, the scythe blades would be bloody with them. Many English settlers left there for the same reason.

With these other Norwegians, the Landsverks organized the Norwegian Lutheran Church on the high hill at Winchester.* Torger and Anne got a very good farm and prospered in America. They had three daughters. One of them married little Tone Daalaan's brother, Halvor.

The letters of Torger and Anne were a fresh sweep of the wind. Oh, this land of America! No more crawling over steep little fields as big as a headkerchief to cut the hay and grain! Here there were gently rolling fields of the blackest, richest soil. One could get 160 acres of it as a homestead for little or nothing. There were tall trees with which to build log houses and barns. Each child could have a great farm and get rich. You must come over before it's all gone. . . . Come over. COME!

The fever took hold of Torger's brother, Halvor Olsson Skare and his wife, Margit. They came to America in 1843, whether before or after Torger, I don't know, and settled in Racine County. In 1853 they moved to Winchester where the rest of the family was gathering. They had three sons, one of whom married Tone Daalaan some years later.

Tone herself left her old Norway at the age of nineteen. Her twenty-two-year-old brother, John, went with her. Tone was the baby of her family, so it made things doubly hard for her parents. She had been the especial pet of her father. He was an old man with long white hair, and she used to stand behind his chair and comb it by the hour. This old father took the youngsters to the sailing boat in Christiania harbor, rowing them out to it, and putting them and their luggage aboard. We still have in the family a little

---

* This church celebrated its centennial in 1950, with a membership of nine hundred.

trinket chest that Tone carried on this voyage. It is about 7 by 3 by 3 inches and is covered with red-and-white plaid paper, closed with a small brass clasp. When the father had bade them farewell, he rowed slowly back to shore. It nearly broke Tone's heart to see that old white head disappear from view, for she knew she would never see him again.

A granddaughter of this old man, named Gro Peterson, we knew later in America. She happened to be staying at the old home in Norway when Tone and John left. She said that when they got out of sight their mother in her agony got down on her hands and knees and crawled all over the floor and prayed and cried for her dear ones. That's how hard it was to see them go off forever. She had already lost two others to America—her oldest daughter Aslaug and the son Halvor.

My mother's and Tone's people seemed to have a great affinity for each other. Many marriages took place between them and their descendents through the years. First, of course, was Mother's oldest sister, Anne Boe, and Torger Landsverk. Later, in America, Tone's brother Halvor married a daughter, Anne, of this Anne and Torger, and her brother John married their daughter, Signe. My brother John married Tone's niece, Isabel, Tone's son married me, and one of our girls married back into the family.

Then there was Aslaug, Tone's older sister, who had been a poor working girl in Norway. She was employed by a very rich family there. The master was a highly respected businessman who had only one son. Aslaug was a winsome girl, with fine smooth features, merry blue eyes, skin as pink and white as cherry blossoms, and a small, delicate figure. It is not to be wondered at that this rich boy became wildly in love with her. Even though in Norway they were great on marrying into families of the same standing, he wanted this poor servant girl for his wife. But she refused, saying that she was below him in station and would always feel ill at ease with his people. But there was another reason for the refusal. My mother's brother, Ole Anderson Böe, had already won her heart. He did not care if she was poor and he wealthy, or that she was ten years older than he. He was so crazed over her that he vowed he "would have her if he had to draw blood." That was how they worded it in Norway. Well, he did get her, and soon after their marriage, they, too, sailed for the new land. They went to the same place as his sister, Anne, and her husband, Torger—to Winchester, Wisconsin.

This Uncle Ole Boe could have carried out his threat, had he not got the girl he wanted. He was a very strongly-built man. One time he and some others had moved a small building by hand. Uncle was so strong that one particular fellow, I am almost ashamed to tell who he was, called him Ole Ox. This name stuck to him. Of course, he felt insulted, and no one ever dared to call him that again to his face. This rascal who called him such a name and was so full of tricks, happened to be my husband's father, Hans. I suppose, as was the style in those days, whenever there was anything extra to be done by a crew of men, they always had to have a few drinks. You can think up a lot of funny things to call people at such times.

It was through this sister and brother that my parents began to think of going to America. There was now quite a colony of our folks in Winchester. Hard as it was to leave home and friends and relatives, they finally made up their minds to sell out and get ready for this long trip. Little by little our relatives had gone, their paths watered with tears of sorrow, and tears dropping into every chest and trunk: sadness in the knowledge that the parting would be forever.

Mother and Father would not leave as long as their parents were living. One by one they had died and were buried with great ceremony. Funerals in Norway were almost as elaborate as the weddings. The ceremony proper, of course, would be at the church and the burial close by. The relatives and friends would not leave the bereaved ones to sorrow alone but followed them home and had a big feast. Not with the jollification that attended weddings, for they were great on "respect," and had too much sympathy for the bereaved.

They would eat sumptuously, however, and there would be plenty to drink for the menfolks, until some weak person would get a little too much, then he would have to be taken home. We were told that one time in Norway, a certain man got sick and died, and the family laid the body out on a bench in an outdoor building until the day of the funeral. Before that day, the man came walking into the house and scared everybody almost to death. They said he had been only "skin dead." He got well, came to America, and lived to be an old man.

THERE WERE few of the immediate family left now to sorrow for our folks when they should leave for the New World. Mother had only one brother in Norway, while Father left three brothers and a sister. Father was fifty-one years old, and Mother thirty-eight. They had seven children, and they could all go along. Ingrid (Anguline) was sixteen years old, Ole fourteen, then Signe, Helga, Andres, John, and Anne, who was three years old.

When they heard that the Civil War was over in America, they packed up their goods. It was in the spring of 1866. There were all their clothes, blankets, spinning wheel, kettles, heirlooms, silver, and numerous household things in the many handmade boxes and chests. One large oak clothes chest that we still have in the family measures 50 by 26 by 26 inches. It is so heavy that two men can hardly lift it empty. The big handles on the sides are of strong wrought iron. It has a rounded top, and is bound all over with fancy iron bands. The enormous lock of iron has a key as long as your hand. On the outside it is covered with *rosemaling* (flower paintings) in faded red, white, and black designs. The background is a soft dark green. On the front are two pretty painted squares outlined in a sort of rope with a loop in each corner. One has the initials HDJ, which I presume were the initials of some Juve, from whom Father bought the farm. In the other square it says, "1816," which is undoubtedly the date of its making.

The inside of this chest is most interesting. On one end is a long box with a lid, a compartment for trinkets and papers. The lid of the chest is bound on the inside with two cut-out iron braces, with red felt padding in heart-shaped designs. This lid is painted a greenish-blue inside, and has the same initials, HDJ, in black on the left-hand side, with "1816" under that. On the right-hand side are the initials JJD, but they have been painted out with the same green-blue paint. Who was JJD? Was this a shipmate, perhaps, from some seafaring days? This stout chest could have stood any voyage. Or was it a wife, perhaps, who had run away from HDJ? It was the custom to call the women by their fathers' Christian names. She could have been a Johanna Johannesdatter. It will always remain a mystery.

Father had another beautifully painted chest, the size of a small trunk. It had "Mathis Olson Juve" written on it in black, painted in handsome script.

The children were ecstatic as they flew to and fro on eager feet, bringing the blankets and clothing to be put in these chests. To think—a trip on a great big sailboat to America! They, who had never been out of their native mountains. How wonderful when they should at last see the dim shores of the great new land! After they had all gone to bed at night, the girls lay with their arms around each other in the darkness, and whispered about the lovely things they were going to see, the handsome men they would meet and marry, the stylish American clothes they would wear. The boys talked of nothing but the great farms they would own, four times the size of these in Norway. But Father, now past fifty, sighed as he looked around at the familiar and beloved scenes for the last times. Mother's tears coursed down her round firm cheeks day and night. They were not like the *fattige* (the poor) who had nothing to leave, and everything to gain in the new land. They were rich and happy in Norway. Why did they have to go? As she laid the wedding guimpe in the chest, she wondered if in America the brides had such pretty things. Taking up the long ceremonial sash and patting it gently into the chest, she repeated softly like a poem the names of the six generations of women who had worn it on their wedding days:

> *Mari Yli*
> *Helga Yli*
> *Thorild Yli*
> *Ragnil Yli*
> *Signe Fröland*
> *Thorild Böe . . .*
> *Farvel . . . farvel . . . farvel . . .*

But there was no time to sit and cry. The boat would sail on a certain day. Passage had been booked; they had to be there. Even though she was with child for the eighth time, she must hurry about and pack the food for that nine-weeks' sailing voyage. It was to be put into the biggest chest of all. This chest was huge but plain, made of maple or birch, painted red. It was about six feet long, as high as one's head, and about three feet wide. To get into it, she opened the lid toward her. It hinged about halfway down the front and was fastened with a hasp at the top. In the bottom were deep bins which reached up to the hinges. In these she put flour, cornmeal, graham flour, and other staples. They must have had dried beef and pickled herring and salted meats and fish. Brother John remembers that there were dried legs of sheep and goats, because there was one leg of this goat meat left when they got to America. He said that one day he and our cousin, John Johnson, found it in the pantry and cut off two big chunks, which they ate in hiding. Above the bins in the bottom of the chest, half-way in depth, was first a shelf lying on the bins, then above that another where she stored butter, cheeses, *flatbröd*, and other things. They said that on the North Atlantic Ocean in April nothing would spoil.

Everybody had been outfitted with new clothes for the journey, of course. The smallest boy, brother John, was not quite six years old at the time. His new suit was of black wool, and there were silver buttons on the pants and coat. But the cap was his pride and delight. It was of brown wool and had a shiny bill—a "boughten cap." And he had new shoes. John was so proud of this outfit that he had to run over to show a neighbor called Old Ole Juve. Old Ole got out his fiddle and played a lively tune in honor of the occasion, bidding John to dance. They were great friends, the old man and the boy. I can imagine that there was sadness in the strains of music that day, mingled with the rhythmic clatter of the little, stiff, new shoes on the bare board floor. They were not to see each other again, these two.

It was in the month of April, 1866, when the day came to load up the wagons, with Father and Mother and all their children high in the seats. Some neighbors went with them as far as Skein, a small port, so that they could take the wagons and horses back when the goods were unloaded. At Skien they were to board a small coastwise sailing vessel that would eventually land them in Christiania, where the ocean-going boat was waiting.

As the family gathered at the wharf in Skien while the sailors loaded their possessions on the little boat, Mother began to count her children. To her horror, one child was missing. It was little John. Everybody began scurrying around, looking behind chests and trunks and casks of fish and overturned boats on the shore. Somebody ran after the departing wagons to see if he had hidden in them. But no! He was not to be found anywhere. Respectable and well-mannered though she was, tears came into Thorild's eyes right there in public. Had her little boy fallen into the sea? But Father soothed her with the thought that the child had probably wandered into one of the sweetshops in town; he would go and look for him.

The sailors began hustling the passengers onto the ship. Mother felt she could not go. Her son was lost! But their passage was bought; all their worldly goods were on that boat. The boat was to go north for one day to pick up other passengers and cargo and then come back, so Father persuaded her to go on board with the other children; he would stay in Skien and search for John and join them when the boat returned.

You can be sure Mother boarded the boat with a heavy heart and that she hardly closed her tear-reddened eyes all that night. She imagined all sorts of terrible things, and finally she came to a conclusion. The *haugetasser* had her boy. These were little mountain people who played tricks on Christian folk. Many a time they had soured the milk overnight in her pans; many a time they had crept into the barns and stripped the cows before morning. Some people thought the *haugetasser* grew up to be *taterer* (gypsies) and now she believed it. This brought on a new burst of tears, and the circle of miserable children sat around her in the cabin and listened to her complaint. All night long she and the children recalled stories of the *taterer*—of how they stole horses, and even children; of the times they came begging to Juve farm, and she had always fed them well; of how Greta Gruba herself, their leader, had come only a few days ago and had cried because the family was going away. That was when they set their eyes on John! Mother was sure of it.

And so it went. Constant talking and weeping while the small, rocking boat nosed in and out of ports, picking up passengers and freight. When the boat neared the Skien wharf again the next day, the whole family gathered on deck, hands shading their eyes. Brother Ole was the first to make out the figures on shore. There was Father! He could tell his hat. And there, hanging his head and hiding behind Father's leg was John, his fine clothes wrinkled and the new shoes dirty. No, he had not been stolen by the *taterer*. He had just gone to sleep on a stable roof. Father assured Mother that he had had his whipping and had learned his lesson. As the family boarded the boat once more, they did not know which emotion was the stronger—joy of reunion or sorrow at leaving Skien.

The sailing ship "Laurdahl," that rode the waves in Christiania harbor, was bigger than any house or church the family had ever seen. It seemed a mountain, this ocean-going vessel, as they clambered aboard. The decks were bigger than a dance floor. Sailors swarmed all over the tall rigging. Soon a wind came up, the sails unfurled, and the boat began to move away from the land which none of them was ever to see again.

It was a stormy voyage, those dreadful nine weeks at sea. Mother never forgot the horror of it. Sometimes the family was very seasick and the food in the tall chest remained untouched. One man drank some salt sea water before he got on the ship, and he swaggered about declaring that that was the way to prevent nausea. But he couldn't get anyone else to try his sickening remedy.

Whenever the weather calmed down, Mother would crawl out of her bunk and cook a good meal. Father would take the rest of the family up on deck for a breath of fresh air. But Mother hardly ever dared go—not unless it was very smooth and sunny. The waves frightened her almost to death, now they seemed as high as the walls of a fjord; now they formed deep caverns that threatened to swallow the ship. So she would remain below and lie in her bunk, and hang on so as not to be thrown out by the motion of the boat.

Little John had not learned his lesson after all. He and Andres were all over that ship. Father had to chase them all day long. Once a big boy snatched John's cap and held it behind his back. As they were tussling for it, the wonderful, bright-billed treasure fell into the sea, and there was no getting it back. Bareheaded and ashamed, and red-faced with anger, John chased the boy until the bully had to hide behind his mother.

John still tells about how he was afraid to go back to the cabin without his cap. Instead, he crawled up on some boxes, clambered along ledges, and got up on the ship's toilet room, where he braced himself behind a board and went to sleep. When he awoke he heard voices. It was his father. "Do you suppose he is up there?"

"Oh, no," a sailor laughed. "No, sir. He could never hang on up there."

"He'd better hang on," another voice added. "If a big wave should come, it could wash him right into the ocean."

John was terrified. As soon as the footsteps had died away, he crept down and made his way to a group of children playing, evading their questions. When evening came he had to go back and face Mother, and he knew that even on a boat in mid ocean she would find some kind of little switch to whip somebody who showed up without his best cap.

ONE DAY THERE was a terrible commotion at the end of the boat. An old man had died, and his horrified relatives heard the captain say that he would have to be buried at sea. A body could not keep, he said, till they got to land. They would make a rough box for him. The family wept and wailed, but it had to be as the Captain said. Now, even while they were getting it ready, a new terror struck. Out of the ocean rose a spouting fish as long as the ship itself. The people could see it churn the water with its tail and turn its black, tarry body over. Mile after mile it followed the ship. The man who had swaggered over his remedy for seasickness now came up from his cabin with a gun. He was going to put a bullet through the creature, but the Captain wouldn't let him. That fish could turn the ship over with one tap of its tail, the Captain said. There was nothing to do but to give it what it wanted.

And so, helpless, they had to stand there and watch the box slide over the rail. The fish was close to the ship's side, its huge jaws open. It caught the box as it struck the water, snapped it in two with one bite, and swallowed the body. Now in his old age, my brother John remembers this moment.

These Norwegians were the sons of Vikings, but such a journey was too much even for them. You can believe there was joy in their hearts and prayers of thanksgiving on their lips when land was sighted one morning. It was Quebec, Canada. From there they went on the Montreal, and, on another boat, even as far as Winneconne, Wisconsin, by water.

On the dock at Winneconne was a wonderful sight. Three of their own people stood there, changed, of course, and older, but their own kin in this strange land. There stood Thorild's brother, Ole Anderson Böe, and his brothers-in-law, Halvor and John Johnson Daalaan. They hadn't seen these two men since they were boys in their teens. What a joyous round of handclasps and huggings. "*Tak Gud, tak Gud.*" (Thank God.) "*Hilse, hilse, hilse!*" (Greetings!)

Only the men were there. The women folk were at home cooking a great dinner. Besides, they needed plenty of space in the wagons. They waited in Winneconne long enough for Ole Böe to do a little trading before starting for home. While Ole traded, Father took John for a walk, holding him, you can be sure, safely by the hand. Halvor went with him. People passing in the street stared at the newcomers; John stared back at the sights he saw.

A fine, prancing horse and shining carriage came alongside them. It was the rich merchant, Tönneson, Halvor said. He had a store in Oshkosh and another here in Winneconne. He stopped his horse and looked at John, then got out of the carriage and came up and spoke to Father. "Is that your boy?" Then he went on to say that he and his wife had no children of their own; they had just adopted a little girl and now they wanted a boy. He actually offered Father a thousand dollars if he would let him have little John. Father was aghast. Was that the way it was in America? Did they sell their own children, their own flesh and blood, here? It was not a good beginning in the new land.

But their sorrows and doubts melted away as they rode along in the summer sunshine, on good solid earth once more. How pretty the land lay before their eyes—black, rolling fields tufted like a quilt with the new green corn. They saw beds of wild strawberries beside the road and clumps of wild pink roses in the corners of zigzag rail fences. Ole Böe pointed with his whip to buildings on a little tree-covered hill—his farm. They could see the women waiting for them.

Thorild could hardly contain herself, lady though she was, when she saw her dear sister Anne, wife to Torger, standing there on the lawn beside Aslaug. How thin Anne felt as she took her in her arms, and how tired she looked! Nobody could say anything for tears. The children tumbled out of the wagons and stood there shyly looking at cousins they had never seen before. They had on such peculiar clothes. But they mustn't stand there keeping "long company" out in the yard, Aslaug said. Dinner was waiting, and everyone wanted to hear the news from home.

And so it began, the lifelong talk about Norway that has never ended to this day.

FATHER AND MOTHER stayed with Anne until they could buy a place for themselves. Torger was now dead. It was terrible to live fourteen in one small log house. And they were not awed by the grandeur of this new country. It did not turn out to be as wonderful as folks had said. Hardships started right away. Then Mother had a baby before the year was out—me, and two more followed. She nearly cried herself to death for Norway. Never having known a day's want in all their lives, now they felt the pinch of poverty wherever they turned. For some reason, they did not settle down on one of the rich, flat farms like their sisters and brothers. Maybe there were none left close by. Father bought a hilly farm, very pretty, but the land was rather sandy and stony. It had a high hill in the middle of it, and a shining, winding creek going through the fields. Maybe it reminded their homesick hearts of Norway. But it was not a get-rich-quick place. Father bought it from a Soren Kjeldalen (pronounced Cheldarn), who had just come home from the Civil War and wanted to start life anew in

Minnesota. The farm already had a log house and a couple of log stables. As small and poor as it was, Father could not pay for it all at once. Farms were much higher after the Civil War than when the other relatives had come over.

Their money was worth very little here in America during those "high times" after the war. Calico was fifty cents a yard, whereas it had once been five; wheat was two dollars a bushel where it used to be about eighty cents. Instead of respecting them as one of the best families of the country, the Yankees laughed at the newcomers and their attempts to speak the English language. They ha-haed right out loud at the embroidered clothing and the silver-buttoned knee-breeches. No wonder Mother and Father did not like this country. After we children had started to go to English school, we would try to talk a little of it at home, but my parents could not stand it. "Go out doors if you cannot talk your mother tongue," they would say.

But despite the hardships, the young folks loved it. They looked out over the broad fields that would be theirs some day and whispered, "Wisconsin, Wisconsin! This is my home."

AMERICA

EVEN THOUGH things were not what my parents had dreamed they would be, there was no time to sit and mourn. Mother and Anguline had to get busy and clean up the log house and make it livable. Father bought a few cows, and now Mother had milk out of which to make cheese and butter. They could not afford to eat these products at first, but traded them for other necessities at the store. Best of all, she had a couple of calves to love and to feed as of old, and a pig and some chickens to tend daily. Father and Ole put in crops right away, but it was a long time before a real income could be got out of this new place.

Mother used to tell with shame what happened to them one day. Having almost no money, they had gone to Winneconne, about seven miles away, and bought a few groceries on credit, something they had never done before in their lives. In a few days the owner of the store drove by and demanded cash. They did not have it, of course. So this man went to the barn and took their best cow and left with it. The best cow, for a fourteen dollar debt! The very thought of it stung Mother all the rest of her life. It did not make her love America any more, you can believe.

They had only gravy to put on their bread for a while. One day Anguline, who was now seventeen and full of spunk, pushed her plate away and said, "I cannot live on gravy any more. I am going out to work." It nearly killed Mother and Father to think of their daughter working as a servant. Not that their children hadn't been taught to work, but none of their family had ever hired out. When Anguline went, Helga (who had changed her name to Hattie) soon followed, and after a few years Signe (who had become Sena). As the boys grew older, they got jobs on near-by farms. Mother wept bitterly for fear the people they worked for would make slaves out of them. She could not see them very often, either, especially if they went as far away as Oshkosh. That was eighteen miles away.

Another thing that worried Mother was her three American-born children. Almost all those born in Norway were tall, and all strong and healthy. I was the first one born here. Although I was never very big, I was as frisky as a young colt and so plump and hard and strong that I could stand anything. I never knew a sick day as a girl, except for a few diseases that swept through the country. But I did not have the Norway stature.

The second child born here was Olena, who became lame as a baby. The third was Kristine, an angel from the start. Never robust, she died at the age of eleven. Mother noticed the difference between her Norway-born children, and these other three, and laid it to the food.* She did not think it healthful to eat white flour all the time. In Norway they ate whole grains except at holiday time. They had much more fish in their Norway diet than here. She did not like the American way of eating, and called it too *feen* (fine).

The third thing that scared Mother to death in this new land was the Indians. She had never seen anything but a white face in all her life. The very thought of these savages turned the whole family pale. If the men were away at work, we were petrified for fear they would find us alone. It happened that our farm was on the Indians' way to the towns where they traded—Oshkosh, Fond du Lac, and others. We could never tell what day they would descend upon us. There never was any warning except the awful pounding of their horses' hooves from the west, up by our neighbor, Nesbitt's. Although we ran and hid, so that there was not a sign of life about the place, they came silently to the door in their soft mocassin feet and would pound on it. Someone would have to go down to appease them for fear they would knock it in, or begin to steal things. It seemed they knew when the menfolks were gone. When we got to the door we would find an Indian man, with black glossy braids over his shoulders and feathers in his hat. His eyes were like black buttons shining between squinted eyelids in his copper-colored face. Dirty he would be, and the hand he held out was filthy. We soon learned what their grunts meant. "Bread!" he would demand. "Pork!" We would peek out and see the company of redskins on the road, seated on their little brown ponies, the women with papooses strapped to their backs. Mother was too scared to refuse them, and we had to share out of our

---

*The parish records of the Winchester church indicate that the infant mortality rate in the early years was high. Of the 67 deaths recorded during the first ten years, 28 were of infants a year old or less—almost 42 per cent.

meager store of food. I suppose the word got around that we were easy marks, for they never failed to stop, and we never got over our fright at each visitation.

These Indians were supposed to come from a place called Waupaca that the Norwegians referred to as *Indie lande*. This was about forty miles away from us. At this place there was a chain of twenty-two lakes, and deep woods all around. Every one of these lakes had Indian names, but when the Indians left, the names were changed to English ones like Rainbow, Long, and Beasley. Only one lake kept the old Indian name, and that was one my husband and I had our summer home on, sixty years later. It was called Lake Menomin. One of their burial mounds was on our farm not far from there, and we could pick up arrowheads all the time.

If the Indians were not going to Oshkosh or Fond du Lac, they might be bound for Butte des Morts (Hill of the Dead). This little town was on a hill by a lake of the same name. They said that there was once a terrible Indian battle there, and that's where the warriors were buried.

One night a man who was working for us came home late. Instead of knocking at the door, he climbed through a window. Mother heard the noise and nearly died with fright, thinking it was an Indian. But it was only Hans Jorgensen.

THE FIRST team my folks had was a yoke of oxen. These faithful animals took the place of horses, which we could not afford. The only bad thing about them was that if they took a notion to run away, there was no way of stopping them, since their mouths were too small to hold bits or reins. The only way to guide them was to holler "Gee" and "Haw" for right and left turns. They were soon trained to know where to go from these orders. You can believe that my proud mother never would ride behind oxen. She preferred to walk.

As soon as Father could scrape together enough money, he bought a team of horses. But the only vehicle we had for years and years was a lumber wagon. On it was one good seat for the driver and next best of kin, usually Mother or Father. There were no springs on the seat, but it bounced on a long hickory beam stretched across the box. The rest of the family would sit behind on plain boards laid across the top of the wagon box, cushioned with folded quilts. We loved these rides, no matter how hard the seats or how rough the roads in those days. We enjoyed getting out in the spring, when the frost was coming out of the ground. It would be so muddy that you could hardly get through in some places. We would have to hang on for dear life where it was bumpy. But we did not know anything better, and we enjoyed it, that is, we little ones. Mother still talked of her two-wheeled cart that went along so fast behind a swift horse in Norway.

Later on, when brother Ole got old enough to take hold of things, we did get a single-seated top buggy, a double-seated buggy, and a cutter for winter. Then you can believe we felt swell.

In the winter the lumber wagon box was put on a pair of bob-sleds. The box was filled almost half full with clean straw, and blankets were laid on top of that. We would sit right down on it, and it was both soft and warm. There were wool quilts over our laps, since we had no fur robes in the early days. Those horses clipped along at a good pace, and we enjoyed a fast ride. In winter the horses had bells on—some strings that reached all around their bellies. Every string had an individual sound. When another team would be coming toward us down the road, we could hear the bells at least half a mile away, and we knew who was coming by the sound. The horses did not have much exercise in winter, so when they had a chance to go, they surely could caper, and the bells would ring and jingle every minute. It was all the driver could do sometimes to keep them from running away. They would prance and jump and gallop for quite a way before they calmed down. We children dearly loved these sleigh rides.

My parents always kept those sleighbells. When I was married and lived in Oshkosh, sometimes I would hear those bells outside the house and go nearly wild with joy, for I could tell whose they were, and know my folks were there.

NOBODY HAD much farm machinery in those early days, and surely not our folks. At the age of fifty-one, Father was really too old to start over, and things did not pick up around our place until brother

Ole was about twenty-one. All we had to farm with were a plow and a drag to break the soil, and a cultivator to keep the weeds out of the crops. The oxen were used for such heavy work. All that the menfolks had to cut their grain with was a cradle, a sort of scythe with four wooden prongs which laid the grain in a neat row. Someone would have to come behind and gather the cut grain into a bundle and tie it. These bundles were laid in rows, too. Toward evening they would be gathered up, and ten or twelve of them stacked into a shock, where they would stay until they were good and dry. Then they could be hauled home and placed in big stacks by the log stables to await threshing time. As soon as I was old enough, this gathering into bundles and shocking was my job.

There were no big barns then, where the grain could be hauled inside. In the fall they would thresh the grain out with a machine that took eight horses to run it. The center of the machine was a big, flat bully wheel on a pinion, from which four strong sweeps made of wood extended eight to ten feet. A team of horses was hitched to each sweep. They were trained to follow each other around and around in a big ring by the signal of a long whip, motioned in the direction they were to go. The man who drove them stood on a platform in the center, over the bully wheel. If one of the horses balked or lagged, he would get a little touch of the whiplash.

Hay was cut with a big scythe, by hand. After it had dried a little, it was raked by hand into windrows, then made into haycocks with a fork. Gleaning was my job. After the hay had cured in the sun, it was hauled to the barn on a wagon and stacked in big stacks. Haying was hard and slow work, but all the farmers had to do the same thing, so they did not expect anything better. People were stronger in those days and could stand a lot of hard work, yet they seemed happier and more contented than people now.

As I said before, there were two log stables when my folks first bought the Kjeldalen farm, one for the horses and one for cows. There was also a sort of shed under a strawstack for the sheep and a little pen for pigs. They didn't keep pigs over winter, except maybe one or two brood sows. The rest would be killed in the fall

39

for winter and summer meat, and for sale. The chickens roosted in the stables.

Mother never got over loving her cows and calves as she had in Norway. In the old country the men did not do chores, but when they got over here, they took over the new-country style of tending to the barn work themselves. Mother still helped with the milking, though, and would not give up taking care of her calves. I have heard it said by some of these hard-working pioneer women that the only rest they had all day was when they sat down to milk cows. Mother never let herself work that hard. But she loved to mix the milk and meal for the calves, and held the pails while they drank and sucked and butted, and they grew sleek and fat under her care. She treated them like individuals and gave every one a pretty name: Kranslin (wreath), Rosebot (rose patch), Stasbot (style patch), Mairose (May rose), Guldbot (gold patch) and Engrose (meadow rose).

There was nothing fancy about either stables or houses among the early immigrants. All buildings were made of logs taken from their own woods. The old log house where I was born is still standing, and it serves as the dwelling house on the farm to this day. It was only 18 by 24 feet square, and you may well wonder how so many people could live in such a small space. Well, they were seldom all there at the same time. The older ones had gone before the babies could even toddle. There were only two rooms and a large pantry downstairs. One of these rooms was a small bedroom for the parents, and the other a large general living room, kitchen, and dining room. Its ceiling was held up by great smooth square beams that shone like glass. Nailed to the bottom side of these beams on either side were shelves. Growns-ups could reach up there to stow away their Bibles, books, mittens, and caps, or anything else they wanted out of the children's way.

The upstairs was all one room. Nobody had partitions, and it wasn't considered necessary. Children were sternly trained in modesty. It was part of their religious belief to keep the body covered, even from one's own sex. Besides, everybody went to bed in the dark and got up in the dark. In winter there would be frost on the quilts, since the roof was open to the peak. We would dress as much as we could under the covers and then make a dash for the stairway, knowing that the old stove in the big room downstairs was giving out a wonderful heat.

Our beds were all made of wood. Instead of side rails there were poles that fastened to four posts. Stout pegs with heads were lodged in these poles. To make a bedspring, all we had to do was to weave a new rope across and back and from top to bottom, hooking it around the peg-heads, until we had five-inch squares over the entire surface. On this rope spring the mattress was laid, and you would be surprised to know what a soft bed it was, for the ropes gave a little with the weight. We strung the rope as tightly as we could, however, so the bed would not sag. Mattresses were of unbleached muslin, filled with clean straw twice a year. Each spring we took these mattresses out, dumped the old straw, washed the ticks, and refilled them with new straw. In the fall we did the same, and believe it or not, those were good, soft, clean beds. But woe to the slack housewife if she ever let bedbugs get a start around those pegs. There was such a dandy place to hatch under the ropes. My mother kept a sharp eye for bugs when hot weather came, and if she ever saw one, she would fly downstairs for her teakettle of boiling water, pail, and mop. Hot water was poured over each peg, and we were never bothered with bugs, as so many people were in log houses.

After many years it got to be the style to pick the inner husks of corn to fill mattresses. These could be used again and again. They had to be emptied out every spring and raked over on the clean new grass to get the dust out. While the mattress cover was being washed and dried, the husks would bake in the sun all day. When they were refilled and laid on the beds at night, it smelled clean all over. I believe those beds were much more sanitary than those we use these days, where the mattresses are used for years and years, and are too heavy to drag out in the sun very often.

The farmers made money out of cornhusks, just as they did other produce. They would bale them and peddle them in the streets of near-by towns, because even town folks used cornhusk mattresses then.

The main article in the big room downstairs was the stove. It stood on high legs, and the dogs and cats took their cozy refuge from the winter weather behind it. Underneath it was very warm, too, and made a good place to thaw out cold feet. We were set up over the fact that the oven was on top of the stove, so that we did not have to stoop to tend to the baking. This oven extended the entire width of the stove, three feet in all. In front of it was a row of four nine-inch covers over the firebox. The ashpit was beneath that again, and in front the sliding grate-shaker. Bowed out in front of the entire stove was the sliding hearth, which could be pushed to one side when the ashes needed raking out. Some of these ashes were saved in a barrel for making soap. There was no reservoir on this stove; we heated water in a big iron kettle. In winter snow was melted in a boiler for washing and cleaning.

Next to the warm, crackling stove in this room, the prettiest and liveliest thing was the big clock on the shelf. It stood about thirty inches high, and was seventeen inches wide. Father had walked to Neenah before I was born, and carried it home on his back. We could never figure out how he could have stood the burden of the two heavy weights all those twelve miles coming home. It is all we can do to lift them now. The weights hung on pulleys on each side of the works; they were what made the clock run. Once a week Father wound them up to the top of the clock with a small crooked crank. This clock is still in perfect running order. Its gong is as musical as when it rang the hours for us in the old log house. Father liked quality in everything. This clock, with its pretty scene of Westminster College on the door, its rose-painted face and fine walnut case, is proof of his love of good things, for it was bought when he was the very poorest of all his life.

The shelf on which the clock stood was bordered in hand-scalloped paper. Immigrants may have had to stick to the bare essentials in most things, but they really let themselves go on the subject of scallops. Sometimes only a newspaper was available, but it was scalloped, or peaked, or pierced in designs. Sometimes the scallops would be of crocheted lace, or bright felt with ribbon running through and a bow in the middle. It used to tickle us children as we were growing up, to see the kinds of "Norwegian scallops" we would find in the different homes.

This shelf, too, held the footed kerosene lamp, where it was out of reach of the children. Mother's little squatty kerosene lamp with the handle, and the chimney that screwed on, was kept on the bedside table in her bedroom.

The only table in this big room was a large square one with drop leaves and an oilcloth cover. If company came, we laid a red-checked cotton cloth over it, but napkins were unheard of. Handkerchiefs were used to wipe our mouths and fingers at table. There were only straight chairs about the room at first. But always in every home there was a long bench against the wall, used for a settee in the daytime, and opened into a bed at night. After a few years we got a couch for Father to take his noonday naps on in this room, since he was getting old.

The window sills in the old log houses were quite deep. There Mother kept her knitting basket, her varnished maple tobacco box, clay pipe, and snuff box. The old ladies used to sniff into their noses a little powdered snuff when they felt stuffy in the head. Maybe there would be less catarrh, sinus trouble, and colds, if snuff were used for that purpose today. Sinus trouble was unheard of in the olden times. Mother did not smoke a pipe after she had been in this country several years. Old Yankee women quit the habit then, and the immigrants had to follow suit or be laughed at.

No one had house plants in the first years, either. But later Mother took to growing flowers in a big way. In those deep sills she would have geraniums, bleeding hearts, chrysanthemums, Jerusalem cherries, wax plants, and many others I have forgotten. She kept them fertilized so richly that they bloomed like a garden. Oh, for just one glimpse of that old sweet home!

After a few years two rockers were bought for our parents. The big one sat in the corner by the hand organ which had been given to Mother by Hattie's husband, Halvor Olson. On a table close by was the stereopticon machine which Halvor had also given her. Halvor was always thinking of something nice to do for people. Mother whiled away many a long hour looking at the views of Norway, and of this big new America, rocking in that old rocker. We children were allowed to look at the stereopticon when we were good. There was one picture of two handsome white mules which used to fascinate us. We had never seen a white mule. They looked so strong, and yet so gentle that you could have put your arms around their necks.

As crowded as this one big room was, every year or so Mother would borrow a loom from one of her kinfolk and set it up. Her sheep had yielded plenty of wool; she had been busy spinning for months. Now her growing family needed cloth for dresses, shirts, and underwear, and more blankets were called for. Sometimes she wove lighter material, with a boughten cotton warp. When she had finished all the weaving, she would dye the cloth with store-bought dye. Things that didn't show, however, like everyday petticoats or mattresses, were dyed with green hazelnut shucks to make them grey, or green hickory-nut shucks for yellowish-brown. But now there was no skilled traveling tailor to be called in to make up the clothes, no tailor to sit and sew all day, and to doze when dusk fell. She had to wait until her grown daughters came home, and they would sew up the cloth in the American way.

All that was in the little downstairs bedroom was a bed, a small stand, and a chair, and a braided rug to stand on when they dressed. Norwegians used two sets of pillows on the bed, filled, of course, with their own home-raised, hand-plucked goose down. The under-pillow was all in one, like a bolster, stretching across the bed at the top. Two smaller ones rested on the bolster. There were many hand-woven blankets and a featherbed for cover, and a pretty hand-pieced quilt for a spread.

Just in front of the pillows there hung a sort of rope attached to an iron eye screwed into the heavy log beam in the ceiling. The lower end had a stirrup-shaped handle. All the way down this rope were little ruffles of red, green, yellow and blue wool cloth, with tiny scallops cut out on the edges. The handle was well padded with bright wool cloth. I do not ever remember seeing this con-traption in any other house, but Mother and Father used it every morning of their lives. They grasped the handle and pulled them-selves up in bed, one at a time. It was especially handy if one happened to be sick.

The remaining room of the house was the pantry, in the south-west corner. It had deep shelves in one corner and over the cellar way. A trapdoor in the floor, with a sunken iron ring for a handle, led to the cellar. Mother's worktable was in the corner under the upstairs stairway, while the washstand (an old backless chair) and grain-sack towel were close by. Mother washed her hands often while she cooked. We used only our homemade soft soap for washing and cleaning and dishes. But for our hands and face and hair, we were allowed the luxury of boughten laundry soap. Toilet soap was a thing unheard of.

Under the worktable in this pantry was the flour barrel, and the big stone crock in which the bread was kept. In winter time the milk and butter were set on shelves, but in summer they would have to be carried down the steep steps to the cellar. All of our food was kept in this pantry or in the cellar, except the hard cheeses and salted meats. These would be kept in the big red food chest brought from Norway. It was too big for the house, so it had to stay in the granary, where no mouse or rat or any other vermin could penetrate its stout exterior.

In this pantry she mixed and rolled out doughnuts and cookies, made bread and biscuits and cheese. Here she set the beer and brewed it in her great copper kettle from Norway. When it had "worked," it was carried down cellar and put in a barrel with a spigot on it.

After a year or so in this country, Father built a little cook shanty to the south of the house. For the log house with its low roof was too stifling hot in summer for a wood fire. When they got a little better off, they built what was ever after known as "the new kitchen," on the south of the house. It was about 18 by 18 feet, and we didn't realize that we were crowded until we got that wonderful extra space. The stove, couch, dining table, and straight chairs were all moved out to the new room. Mother got a fine cupboard with screens on the sides and doors. Here she could store food and dishes away from flies and mice. Her worktable and flour barrel were moved out, too, and the washstand, towel, combcase and mirror. In summer we washed just outside the west door.

On the east side of the new kitchen we even built a porch, where there were benches and chairs on which to sit and cool off on a hot day. Here in the summer evenings brother Ole would sit and play his violin by the hour, tune after tune of the Norwegian folk songs and dance music, without stopping in between. It would make the old folks sit and sigh for happy days in their Old-Country home. But we little ones would slip off with tingling feet to try some of the new American dances we had caught glimpses of now and then.

COOKING

WE HAD SO MUCH company in those early days that Mother had to spend a great deal of her time cooking. She had to be prepared at all times for a visitor, and no one ever went away without a meal or a "treat" of some sort. Though the folks were poor, they still carried on the same hospitable traditions of Norway.

The new kitchen was a tremendous help to Mother. It was so handy and cheery in there. She even had a new stove by and by, with a reservoir on the side. The wood fire shone through the cracks in this new polished stove, and the copper teakettle bobbled its lid and whistled merrily on top. King Coffee Pot, in iron grey and shining helmet, guarded the tasty brew near the reservoir at all times.

Mother's long blue gingham dress swung back and forth in the cook corner as she began to fix the bread. This white yeast bread was something she had to learn to make in America, but she became so expert at it that her fame spread all over the township. She was a natural-born cook, anyway, and so neat and clean with it that people loved to come there. The bread sponge would be set in the afternoon. This consisted of the potato water left from dinner, and woe to the one who carelessly tossed it out during the dish-washing. Into this water she mashed a few left-over potatoes. Then she put in an old-fashioned dry yeast cake, which had been soaking in lukewarm water. She sprinkled in some salt and sugar, according to the judgment of her practiced hand, and thickened it with flour until it was a little stiffer than pancake batter.

Now this precious sponge in its crock would be wrapped in a clean flour-sack towel, and then in an old white woolen skirt. It would be set on a wooden board on the back of the reservoir to keep warm.

In the evening the big sponge was set. She put lukewarm water in the large *brödtraag* (bread trough) which Father had hollowed out of a log. This he had scraped with a piece of glass until it shone like glass inside. The bread kept warm longer in a wooden trough, than in a metal one, and would rise better. An eight- or ten-loaf batch of bread would take about three quarts of water. To this the sponge was added. With a good stout wooden spoon that Father had also carved for her, she stirred in the flour and gave it all a vigorous beating. Then the clean flour sack, woolen skirt, and pieces of old red blanket were tucked about it, and it was put to bed on a backless chair behind the stove.

In the morning when she opened it, the top was covered with bubbles working as if it were alive. The tingling yeasty odor filled the kitchen. Now she had more sifted flour warmed and ready, which she added with more salt and sugar, and began to knead with all the strength of her stout arms, until the dough was as light as a feather. It must then rise to the top of the trough, when she would tackle it again with might and main. After this last punching it would be bundled into blankets once more, when it would presently fly up to the top of the trough. In the meantime, she had her tins greased with pork-fryings, and as soon as it had risen the second time, she would cut off a piece big enough for a loaf, deftly form it and lay it in the tin. In no time the loaves had swelled to their full capacity, and just as they were about to roll over the sides of the tins, she would put them into the hot oven, where they stayed until they were baked a golden brown. When they came out of the oven, she greased the crust with pork-fryings again, and turned them on edge on a clean breadboard, which had been scrubbed snowy white with sand.

Now all the time it was baking, we children had been getting more and more eager, and our mouths would fairly drip from all the delicious aroma in the kitchen. As soon as one loaf got cool enough, we would begin to beg for a slice. Mother would take up her sharp bread knife and slice into one of the crispy loaves, crumbs flying in brown flakes all over the board. On it she would spread generous slabs of homemade butter, and maybe a slice of *gammelost* (old cheese) and shoo us outside with a pleased smile on her face.

This is how Mother made her butter. When the milk came to the house in pails, she would go with it to the pantry and lift up the ponderous *kjellarlem* (trapdoor), taking it by its big iron ring, and lean the door carefully against the wall. To keep from falling into the hole, she would grasp the shelf above it with her other hand. Then sitting carefully down on the edge of the hole, she sought sure footing on the heavy hand-hewn ladder. Grasping the top rung, she would swish her skirts in after her. Halfway down the ladder she would stop, and hanging on to a rung, take a long, fearful look around the cellar. She did this to make sure that there were no *orms* lurking around, crawling along the window ledge or slinking along the floor. This pause was in remembrance of the terrible morning long ago when she actually did find an *orm* sliding along the floor, which sent her up to the trap-steps in a hurry, hollering for "Mathis." It was only a harmless little green snake, which probably rued the day when it had fallen through the window. But an *orm* was an *orm* to Mother. They were all serpents from the Garden of Eden, and creatures of evil.

After she had made sure that the cellar was safe, she would call to Mathis to lower the pails of milk. These she strained into sweet, scalded shallow milk pans, and set them in shining rows on a long shelf. Now was the time to take the skimmer and skim off the cream from the two-day-old pans. The cream was gathered into a two-gallon crock, and the remaining skim milk poured into the pails for the calves and pigs out in the barn. Then everything would be handed up to the patient waiting Mathis.

The tall stave churn which had been scrubbed and scalded thoroughly and had stood long hours with the hot sun pouring into its mellow golden well, was trundled out from its own corner in the pantry to the warm kitchen. There it was filled with coldest water from the well, to match the temperature of the chilled cream, and the dash handle would stick crazily out of the top. Mother, who seldom had to pump any water, emptied this churn water right out on the ground, and poured her jars of thick gobby cream into the churn in its place. Father now sat in the shade outside, and it was his job to churn rhythmically and steadily until the butter gathered in yellow islands all over the buttermilk. At this he would set up a glad call. *"Thorild, kom, naa har eg smör!"* ("Thorild, come. Now I have butter!") She would come smiling, with a butter ladle and bowl hugged against her round stomach, pleased that the cream had been so nice as to give up its butter so quickly. She also dangled a tin cup in one hand, so that her beloved Mathis might have his reward in all the buttermilk he could *orka* (hold).

While he was drinking and smacking his lips, and wiping the

white moustache of buttermilk off with the back of his hand, Mother gathered the butter into a lump and put it into her bowl. Over and over again she worked the butter in fresh water, until the water finally came off clear. The butter was then salted with old-fashioned barrel salt until her taste said it was enough. Then she packed it into jars, tied a little cloth over the top, and covered it with a plate. After saving out a generous supply for her family, the remaining jars were put in the pantry to be lowered into the cellar. There they awaited the market day, when they would be traded for coffee, flour, sugar, or even clothes at the village store.

CERTAIN ACTIVITIES took place in the fall of the year, in preparation for the long Wisconsin winter. Mother still had a woman come to make the winter's supply of *flatbröd*. She was a Marta Johnson, who travelled from house to house performing this task. It would take her many days to get enough put by to last till spring.

After they got in a little better circumstances, the folks continued to butcher as much as they had in Norway—four or five small pigs in the fall, a beef, and the lambs in the spring. The best of the pork would be salted down and the remainder made into blood sausage, head cheese, and *syltre* (pickled pigs' feet), liver sausage, and meat sausage made from the scraps, flavored with salt, pepper, and thyme.

When they butchered a beef, the best part would be made into corned beef to eat in the summer. This was done by putting it down in brine in big crocks. In winter the bones were used for soups. These had been salted just a little and kept in the chest in the granary, for they would not be kept over till warm weather. The stew meat was kept in brine, later to be cooked up with potatoes, carrots and onions. As the time went by and the old folks began to lose their teeth, Mother made more and more food that required little chewing. My parents were never sick until their last illnesses at the ages of ninety-three and ninety-five, which attested to the soundness of Mother's feeding and caring for the sturdy bodies they had inherited.

We had soups of all sorts. One of them was a fruit soup which we liked very much. It was made of barley or rice, raisins, prunes and grape juice, sweetened to taste. The grape juice was some she bottled herself every summer. Fruit soup was a supper dish and was eaten with bread and butter, or perhaps with cookies for dessert. A lot of breadstuffs gave heat and energy in that brisk Wisconsin climate.

Mother's greatest fame, however, came from the way she made cheese. You may know that anyone who had gone to a *seter* in Norway from childhood could be counted upon to know her business in that line. She made a wide variety of cheeses and they formed an important part of our diet. I think some kind of cheese was on the table every meal of our lives.

Sweet cheese (*södost*) was made out of whole sweet milk. Milk was heated on the stove in a copper washboiler to blood warmth, then she added rennet which she had made from calves' stomachs. It was cut in little pieces, put in a muslin bag, and dropped into the milk, causing it to curdle. When the curds were gathered in lumps about the size of one's little finger, she skimmed them out and salted them. Into a clean flour sack they went, then into a vessel to be pressed under the weight of a big, clean stone to remove the whey. It was then put away in a cool place to ripen for a few weeks, when it was considered ready. Off would come the sack, and the round cheese, now firm and of smooth texture, would delight the eye and cause the mouth to water in anticipation. A triangle would be cut out of this smooth cheese to be sliced at table. How good it was, laid on top of Mother's delicious bread and butter! When this *södost* got old and hard, Mother cut it in chunks and put it in brine, when it would turn green and yellow in places. This was the time that Ole Stromme, an old neighbor, would say,

> *Ja naar osten blir saa gammel*
> *At den er gul og grön,*
> *Da er den god!*

> (When the cheese is so old
> That it is green and gold,
> Then it is good!)

This green and gold cheese could be kept all winter in the big wooden food chest in the granary.

The whey from this sweet cheese was put into the big copper kettle and hung on a strong pole laid on the old-fashioned fireplace out in back of the cook shanty. Father had made this fireplace of field stone and mortar, and it was known as the *"eisa."* It was circular, about thirty inches high, with a place cut out in front to put the wood in. The whey in this copper kettle was cooked all day, and it had to be stirred many hours with a *sleiv*, a great, long, wooden spoon with a flat bowl about five inches wide, which Father had made. It was Father's job to stir the whey to keep it from sticking to the bottom of the kettle, and to keep the fire going with fat tamarack chips and stout oak chunks. When the *prim* (whey cheese) was cooked down about as thick as apple butter, the fire was allowed to die down, but still the mixture had to be stirred until it got cold. One had to stand up to do this stirring. Father would be relieved now and then by Mother, or one of the children, who took to the task with unwilling hearts, but we never dared to demur, for Mother's tongue was as sharp as a splinter. After the *prim* was cold, it was put in crocks, sealed with melted butter, and a clean rag tied around the top, then more paper to keep it clean. An old plate was put on top of the paper to keep out the mice, who were as fond of Mother's cheese as we were.

When the time came for the *prim* to be used, it was dished out with a strong spoon, enough for a meal at a time. If one didn't like it dry, it could be boiled up with a little water and sugar and restored to freshness. Or it did not need to ripen at all, but could be spooned out of the crock and mixed with cream and sugar, and spread on bread and butter. This way it was a summer spread. If it was to be saved for winter, it was cooked somewhat longer, and shaped into dry hard balls, and laid in a dry place.

But chief of all the cheeses was *gammelost* (old cheese). Any Norwegian, near or far, will smack his lips and take a deep breath at the sound of the memorable word.

The first step in making *gammelost* was to make cottage cheese out of clabbered sour milk. It was put at the back of the cook stove in an iron kettle and allowed to stand with a few stirrings, until the curds rose to the top in a smooth mass. This was skimmed off and put into a clean cloth, and hung up on a hook over a table, with a pan set under to catch the whey. The whey from *gammelost* was too small and sour a portion for *prim*, for which the pigs in the barnyard were very glad. They would stand with their front feet in the trough and squeal at the top of their voices when they smelled it coming.

Now you could stop here and have cottage cheese for supper, by mixing the curds with salt and cream. However, if you wanted *gammelost*, it was first hung longer, so as to get it very dry. Then it was crumbled fine between the hands and put into a stone pan, a hole scooped in the middle of it and the cheese pushed to the side of the pan. A clean cloth was put over it, and then it was let to stand in a warm place, sprinkled with water every day until it began to "work" and smell rotten. Then the cloth was removed and a little water poured on it. Caraway seed and salt were added to taste, and you could eat it right away on bread and butter, when Norwegian noses, tongues, and hearts were most satisfied. Or you could put it away in a covered jar, for the longer it stood, the more *gammel* (old) it got, and the more tantalizing to the nose, which had so much to do with the enjoyment of this delicacy. When it ran together in a greyish, flecked mass and smelled strong enough to knock you back down the cellar steps, it attained the height of the genuine and highly-prized *appetitost* (appetite cheese). More could not be expected of food on earth. Then it was almost revered, as was due its age and excellence.

Another way to fix *gammelost* before it got too old, was to put it in a pan and boil it with a little milk and caraway seed, when it would turn a glossy grey. It was poured in a jar to cool, whence it could be cut in nice shiny slices. *Gammelost* was too powerful to keep. The worms found out about it after just so long a time. So it was made frequently both summer and winter.

There was one old couple, Jon Westgaarden and his wife, Aslaug, that used to come to our house a lot. They were old friends from Norway. Mr. Westgaarden was exceedingly polite to his wife, and you would think that they had not been married more than six months. When they were at our house, we children would nearly burst to see and hear him. He could never taste anything at the table until he had first passed it to Aslaug, and recommended it to her earnestly. Mother's cheese was famous among the Norwegians, because she made it exactly as they did in the old country. When Jon would pass the cheese to his wife, he would say in a tremulous voice (in Norwegian, of course), "Oh, Aslaug, you must have some of this good chee-ee-eese!" Just as though she had never heard of *gammelost*, or tasted it before. Children never ate at the table with grownups in those days when there was company, but would sit around the big room and wait their turn. When this man began his "Have some of this good chee-ee-eese!" we would sidle out the door and get out of sight so that we could burst out laughing. If Mother ever had caught us at it, so that the company had heard us, we would have been whipped good.

This man was also a great singer. After dinner, the old folks would sit back and talk while the children ate and washed dishes, and after they had satisfied themselves about old times in Norway for another time, he would take up the hymnbook and sing. Then it was time for us children to look out for a handy door again. For at the end of each verse, he would push the book out in front of him, raise his eyes to the ceiling and draw out a trembling note. One look from Mother would send us out the door.

Mother's cookie jar was never empty, either, and anyone could have a cookie at any time as long as he didn't spoil his meal with it. The big, round, crisp cream cookies were stirred up like lightning by Mother, who kept the recipe in her head. She would cream a few pork fryings and sugar, add eggs and cream and flour and nutmeg, and before you knew it she had them in the oven. In about ten minutes they would come out, sparkling with the sugar she had sprinkled on top, and their aroma tingled in the nostrils. She had to keep a generous supply on hand, because we had company at all hours, and every comer was offered coffee. The lump sugar bowl was never empty, either. A lump was dipped in the coffee and sucked noisily with satisfaction, accompanied by cream cookies. This happened five times a day. The coffee pot never left the stove. There was a kind of Peaberry coffee which Mother loved. When it was poured steaming hot into the oversized ironstone cups, thick lumps of cream were poured in after.

Desserts were not much in use at our house. We got our sweets from a little rock candy which was kept up in the screen cupboard and dispensed for good behavior. In summer and fall Mother prepared apple sauce by cutting the fruit, removing the blossom end and stewing it with sugar and a little water. After many years in this new country, the women began to do a little canning. They learned to make different kinds of pickles, which added a tart flavor to our winter meals. Mother's favorites were green tomato pickles, sweet ripe cucumber pickles, and chow-chow. She used to make gallons of that, and put it down in stone jars. Sweet crab-apple pickles were a treat, too, and crab-apple jelly and plum jelly. As the years went on and the apple orchard that brother Ole set out began to bear, there was plenty of applesauce to liven up the winter fare.

People appreciated Mother's cooking, and never failed to tell her so. Our neighbor, Ole Stromme, when he rose from a meal at our house, never forgot to say, "This was the best meal I ever ate in my living time." To which Mother, bursting with pride, would rock her head from side to side and reply modestly, "*Aa nei, det var ikkje so svært.*" (Oh, no, that was not so great.) But she could not conceal a very pleased look on her face. She might not have been able to bring with her the riches that were hers in Norway to this raw new land, but she could bring her skill and her open hands and heart. These no one could take away from her, no matter where she went.

All the time her adoring Mathis would look up at her with a loving smile and nod his head to agree with Mr. Stromme, saying, "*Ja ja ja. Det var god, Thorild.*" (Yes, indeed, it was good, Thorild.)

Our house was not too unusual in respect to cleanliness and hospitality, although I believe Mother was the best cook in the neighborhood. Everybody kept a neat house, and bounteous meals could be set before company at short notice.

One exception to this rule was Anne and Torger's youngest daughter, Maria. Anne had been so fond of her that she had spoiled her. When Maria married, she had children so fast that she did nothing but tend to them, and they were so fat and pretty that it was a sight to see. But she couldn't be bothered about the house.

When you came to see Maria, her arms reached out in the heartiest welcome, and there was not the slightest embarrassment on her part if the house was in a mess. She would be so glad to see you that she would hasten to clear out a chair and dust it with her apron, and then you must sit right down and tell her all the news, while she would tell you hers.

There wouldn't be a thing to eat in the house, but that didn't bother Maria a bit. While she visited with you, she got out her stave churn, poured in some cream, and set it beside her chair. As the dasher went up and down, it kept time with her cozy chatter. Pretty soon she would have butter, and would work up a generous pat for the table. With the buttermilk she would make the most delicious soda biscuits you ever tasted in your life. These she would set on the table by the butter pat, and set on a dish of elegant tomato or plum preserves. With these went cups of steaming hot coffee, floating with thick cream. Visitors somehow went away from Maria's house feeling that they had had a kingly meal.

CHURCH

THE LUTHERAN CHURCH at Winchester was on a high hill about two miles away from our farm, and Sunday would find all of the grownups and children there, except the little ones who could not walk that far. Our folks were always there. They had been well supplied with Norwegian clothes when they came here, both for everyday and Sunday. They soon found out, however, that the style and cut of knee breeches with silver buttons, rich embroidered guimpes, and brightly-banded skirts caused laughter wherever they went. So, despite their financial troubles, they had to change over to American style as soon as they could. This was hard, because they had been accustomed to the best, and the best clothes were expensive after the Civil War.

Saturday night was bath night, but you must not think that we had reached the stage where we took tub baths every week. That still occurred only before Christmas and Easter. But our folks all took a weekly sponge-bath on Saturday night, and loved a clean body smell.

Sunday was no time for extra sleeping. We got up between five and six o'clock and put on old clean everyday clothing until the work was done. Just as little as possible was done on Sunday, for all the cleaning and baking and other work had been finished on Saturday. The menfolks would go out to do the chores while Mother made coffee, set the table, and fried the pork sausage. When Father had done his chores, he would come in and sit by the table in his armchair and read the prayer for the day, singing the hymn that went with it. *Morgen og Aften Betragtninger* (Morning and Evening Devotions) was the name of the book. He had carried it with him from Norway.

At breakfast he would first have one of Mother's good cups of Peaberry coffee, made rich golden tan with lumps of cream. Next he would reach for one of her thick slices of bread and cut it in lengthwise strips, then crosswise, making cubes. Upon each of these he would lay delicious yellow butter, almost as thick as the bread, and eat each cube with a smack of his lips. We children couldn't wait to go to all this trouble, but bit hungrily from the big slices. We would all enjoy the sausage and *prim* and crisp sugar cookies, and of course, the grownups would have cup after cup of

61

hot coffee. We children drank water. With all that milk around, you would have thought they would have fed us that, but it never seemed to occur to them. We just didn't drink sweet milk as a beverage, but we had plenty of it with *gröt*, in cooked food, in cheese, and as clabber.

There would be a great bustle getting the breakfast dishes done before we dressed for church. Then the dressing would start, and there was no monkey business, for we had to walk that two miles and had to be on time.

By the time I was old enough to take notice of things, Father had two elegant boughten shirts, of the purest fine white cloth and American make. They were used only for church, funerals, weddings, and other special events. The lot of doing up these shirts usually fell to the daughters of the family when they were home, for Mother was too busy cooking and tending to her calves to bother with them. The shirt bosom had to be starched as stiff as a board. The shirt was full and wide and long, buttoned down the back. Father never wore an American collar with these shirts, but tied around his neck instead a fine brownish silk neck scarf, knotted in front. They were kept in a special *skuff* (drawer) in the *dragkiste* (chest with drawers).

He had one best Sunday suit, of the finest black wool; this was seldom pressed but was brushed carefully after each wearing, folded in the original creases, and laid away in a trunk upstairs.

His Sunday shoes were plain, broad-toed, laced, black calfskin, which he greased, both soles and tops, with unsalted lard every Saturday. Summer and winter he wore woolen stockings which Mother knit for him, lighter in weight in summer, and not quite so long as in winter. They were held up with a buckled leather strap. A medium-brimmed black felt hat with a round top sat upon his fine black shoulder-length hair, which was now streaked with grey. In his pocket would be a big, clean, white handkerchief. He carried in his hand a large leather hymnbook with two brass buckles on it. This was the *Landstads Psalmebog* (Landstad's Hymnbook). Old Pastor Norby said once of him: "As long as this old faithful servant of the Lord could crawl to the altar, he came regularly to communion, and that was until he was ninety-two years old."

Mother's dressing would go like this: First, next to the skin went a long bandage, wrapped tightly about the abdomen, cotton in summer, wool in winter. This was her corset, and she was never without it. Over that would go a clean white shift of sturdy cloth. Then a full tan cotton petticoat with a border of many colors around the bottom, red and green and brown. This was topped by a pretty white cotton petticoat with lace or embroidery at the bottom, about two or three yards around. Her dress was of black alpaca with tight-fitting waist and full skirt, tight-fitting sleeves, and a little black collar around the high neck, fastened with a black bone pin in the shape of a four-leaf clover. Black jet buttons closed the front and the sleeves.

Mother was a fanatic on hair-parting. No comb could do the job. We could see her go to the small mirror in the kitchen with a steel knitting needle, and draw a perfect line straight down the middle of her head. I could never understand why she was so particular about this, for her head was always covered. For everyday she always wore a three-cornered scarf, and for church a bonnet. After parting the hair, she drew the two parts smoothly to the sides, rolled them into a plain round pug low on her neck and fastened them with steel hairpins. On top of this hair-do, she tied a black silk bonnet, trimmed decorously with black laces and ribbon, with a black or white ruching around the face, and a wide bow under the chin. One of us children would be dispatched upstairs for her black cashmere summer shawl, the point of which fell just long enough for her to sit on it. This was fastened with a long, black-headed pin. In winter, the dark red shawl, being heavier, was held together with two bigger silver pins, hooked together with a chain. These pins were topped by a small silver cup, each filled with a pretty blue stone.

Mother wore black cotton gloves on her big shapely hands. These gloves hid all evidences of the toil which was her earthy lot. Her thumbnails were always rough and dark-streaked, of which she was very sensitive. All the Sunday clothes smelled of cloves and withered sweet apples, kept in her chests for perfume. There would often be a smell of camphor about her, too, for that was her chief medicine. The deep pockets sewn in the seam of the right side of her skirt would contain a clean handkerchief, and several cloves and peppermints to keep her breath sweet in God's house.

Mother's favorite hymnbook was of brown leather with brass buckles, rather long and narrow. She would as soon have gone to church without her bonnet as without that book.

It was very pleasant going to church, walking along the road. First we climbed the high hill at the edge of our farm, and as soon as we reached the top, a fresh breath of wind would strike our cheeks, flushed from the climb. The air was as clear and sunny and quiet as Sunday should be, with no "Gee" or "Haw," or "Whoa" and "Giddap" from the fields, as on weekdays. Cows moved along slowly in the pastures beside the road, snatching off tufts of clover and munching as they watched us, purple blossoms bobbing up and down on either side of their swinging jaws. Now we passed the Houghs, our English neighbors, who were hitching up their double-seated buggy to go to church in Mikesville. The wind blew my long flowered Dolly Varden dress against my black-stockinged legs, and the dust gathered in annoying layers on the round toes of my newly-greased, black, high-buttoned shoes. I had to hang on to my wide straw hat, even though it was tied under the chin. My thick red braids felt hot against the perspiration gathering at the hairline.

Brother Ole walked solemnly at the head of the procession, hymnbook under his arm, scanning with squinting eyes the progress of the neighbors' crops on either side of the road. The other older girls and boys had long since gone out to work, or to be married, and were home only for short vacations. So our family was small.

Mother and Father came next, with Kristine holding onto Mother's black-gloved hand. Every now and then the child would turn her delicate pink and white face up to Mother, and we could see the brown lashes lying against her eyelids as she raised those sky-blue eyes to look at her. Could she have a peppermint when they got to church? Would it be all right if she sat with Father on the other side this time, so that they could sing together the hymn he had taught her? Mother smiled down at her tenderly and explained that a big girl like her had to sit on the women's side. It wasn't *skikkelig* (decent) for her with the men. Kristine sighed.

64

Olena, the lame sister, who would fix you if you pronounced that O, usually trailed behind with me. Despite the lame leg, which was drawn up behind the knee so that she had to walk on the toes of that foot, Lena could get around remarkably well, and walked and ran nearly as much as the rest of us. She looked healthy, too, with a round rosy face, and big blue eyes that saw everything, especially everything funny. Her thick blonde hair was drawn back and braided at the top of the head, then caught in another braid with a ribbon that bobbed at the back edge of her wide, yellow straw hat. Lena and I often dressed alike, in dresses that our older sisters made and sent us after they got to working. Mother never got the hang of making fashionable American clothes. The older girls did all our sewing until we were old enough to do it ourselves.

These dresses of Dolly Varden cloth were our summer favorites —white background with red roses and green leaves that never faded. The skirts were so long and full that the ruffle around the bottom reached our shoe tops. The waists were small and tight, and buttoned down the back. Little collars came close around the necks; the sleeves were long with ruffles at the wrists. Nobody ever wore short sleeves and low necks in our day. In winter it was too cold. In summer you might get tanned.

Lena and I had many good laughs as we walked along to church. Just before we got to Peder Lund's house, we could see him driving out of the farmyard with his wife, Bergit, seated beside him in the open buggy. She was a tall woman, and since he was a short hunchback, he barely came up to her shoulder as they sat. Lena and I giggled about the time his stepdaughters hitched up that horse and buggy and drove it to the house, getting ready to go somewhere. Peder, who was full of fun, plucked his wife by the sleeve and hustled her into the buggy while the girls were dressing. He drove off at a gallop, laughing over his shoulder as the astonished girls came tumbling out of the house. We saw these same girls now coming out of the back door to walk to church. Peder had to be there early, because he was *klokker* (sexton) and had to ring the bell.

As we turned the corner at Mott's schoolhouse, we looked over our shoulders down the road to the south to see Aunt Anne and her flock coming, and waved at them. I never saw the tall Torger. He had died years before. Aunt Anne had even been married a second time, but the marriage didn't last long. Soon after the wedding, the second husband had been kicked by a horse at Mathis Mathisen's and killed.

On our way to the big Winchester hill, Lena and I had another giggle. One of the Norwegians whose house we passsed was a terrible drunkard. He was also possessed with a great desire to fiddle while he drank. One night when he was pretty full, and was fiddling for all he was worth, he saw the Devil come in the door and bend over him. The poor man flung the fiddle down right then and there and never took it up again. Norwegians have a most awful fear of the Devil.

The church dominated the entire countryside. For miles you could see the seventy-five-foot, grey-shingled spire with the bell hanging in it. The sweet, rich tone of that six-hundred-pound bell reached the farthest member of the congregation in his home, calling him to worship. It had been given by the young people of the congregation. In this country, as in Norway, people were very faithful to their church. Even before we had reached Mott's corner, we had seen the red brick walls of the church, with its arched windows, shining through the green leaves of the trees that surrounded it, and streams of people walking along the road toward it. As we trudged up the hill, we could see the upper stories of the red brick parsonage across the road from the church, and then as we rounded the top, the graveyard with its few white marble slabs above green mounds beside the church.

Now we could see groups of people before the steps, shaking hands, bonnets bobbing and hats nodding as the friends and relatives saw each other for the first time since last week. "*God dag, god dag, god dag*" (good day) we heard on every side. Just before we joined them, Mother looked back over her shoulder, and bending her stern grey eyes on us, said, "Remember what I told you. You shall be 'folk' in church." By this she meant that we weren't even people if we couldn't behave in God's house.

In the dim church doorway Peder was reaching for the thick bell rope. He looked like a gnome out of our schoolbooks, hunch-

66

backed and small, his long, black beard rising and falling on a white shirt bosom as he tugged on the rope, the fierce black eyebrows bent in earnest. The great clanging of the bell pounded on our eardrums, and there was no peace from it until we moved with the sea of black trouser legs and full skirts into the vestibule.

The interior of the church was cool and quiet. The light that came through the frosted glass windows did not have the brilliance of outdoor sunshine but a soft, golden, hallowed glow instead. From the ceiling hung fancy kerosene lamps in sets of four, whose fat, frosted chimneys had fluted tops. There was a swinging bracket lamp beside the pulpit. On each side of the church paneled posts supported a huge square beam. Seats behind these posts were coveted by the young people, who could make eyes at the opposite sex across the aisle, unseen by the preacher.

The chancel was divided in two parts, with the altar in front of and the vestry behind the partition. The *altertavle* (altar painting), in soft reds and blues and greens, was of Christ on the Cross and his Mother. The lower panel was of the Lord's Supper. Beneath that was the altar itself, where the congregation laid the money when offering time came. This altar was covered with a long, white, lace-edged cloth, and on this stood two tall, footed, silver communion goblets. In front of the altar was a raised half-circle of red-carpeted floor, and a railing all around it with a red-carpeted kneeler before it. On this people knelt when they went to communion, when they were confirmed, and when they were married. In front of this railing the coffins were placed during the funerals. On either side of the altar at the back a door led to the sacristy, and over each door an arch of pale blue with a verse of scripture lettered in gold. One of them I can remember: "He that believeth and is baptized shall be saved." The baptismal font, where all the American children of our family were baptized, was at the front, by the reed organ.

Men and women divided when they entered the church proper, men to the right, women and children to the left. Aunt Anne came in, a little out of breath and sat beside us. There were so many Annes, Aslaugs, Oles, and Johns in our relationship that the Totingers (people like Peder Lund from Toten, Norway) started the style of linking the people to their mates' names. So this Aunt Anne was "Anne to Torger." She was a little frail woman, with a tired face and black rings under her eyes. And she sat bent over, as if her chest were crushed. Those stooped shoulders she had acquired in her first days in America. They had no well on their farm, and she had to get her drinking and cooking water from Rogers' Spring, a quarter of a mile away from her house. To help her carry two pails at once, Uncle Torger had fashioned a wooden shoulder-yoke for her. Mother used to shake her head at this. She and Anne had not been raised to carry water on a shoulder-yoke like an ox. Father never would let Mother carry a pailful even from the well in our yard to the house, but kept her supplied at all times. Torger was not mean to Anne; he was just not as careful with her as the men were at our house.

"Aslaug to Ole Böe" was there, with her three lovely daughters, Anne and Signe and Gurina. Anne was my special friend, and remained so all her life. Signe and Gurina were older and had already changed their names to American ones. Signe became Sena, Gurina became Julia, but the old folks disregarded their whims. These three girls were as fine featured and stylish as their mother, with twinkling blue eyes and rosy lips, held demurely in church. Uncle Ole Böe sat across the aisle, his rough hands folded on his great strong knees, his balding head with grey hair combed back, his thick, sunburned neck bent. Aunt Aslaug's sister Tone did not go to this church but to another down the road which I shall tell you about later. I was glad of that, because she had a boy, John, who was always staring at me.

Peder Lund got up again from his front seat and with a tremendous but melodious voice announced, *"Vi skal synge nummer saa og saa."* (We shall sing Number so and so.) What a relief to our cramped legs to stand and sing! Kristine knew this hymn. We could see her looking up at the *altertavle* as she sang. I wished I could be as angelic and enjoy church as much as that little thing.

After a certain amount of ceremony and singing, the minister appeared as if by magic in the window-high pulpit at the right front, which was called the *predikestol* (preaching chair). It was attached to the wall, and was paneled and carved, with a padded red velvet railing around the top. Pastor Homme was a great, stout Martin Lutherish man, in a long black robe, with a starched white ruff coming up to his clean-shaven chin. He had a large expanse of forehead with a tuft of hair curled in a baby-roll toward the middle back. His broad cheeks were flanked on each side by a clump of sideburns, and the nostrils of his big handsome nose expanded and contracted from the little climb up the steps to the pulpit. His keen blue eyes looked over the house from beneath the brown brows, and Lena and I sat back in our seats, frozen. Pastor Homme could see things, and we would hear of it afterwards. He grasped the red velvet railing with his great smooth hands, and leaned forward as he preached, searching our eyes with his in earnest pleading and warning. If anybody went wrong in that church, it wasn't because the pastor had neglected his duty or hadn't set a fine example of Christian living. His sermon was long and in "book Norwegian," which was hard for Lena and me to understand. We were glad when it was over and we could go home to dinner.

THIS PASTOR HOMME served our congregation fourteen years. He was not married when he came to Winchester, but his sister kept house for him. Our neighbor, Ole Stromme, was a particular friend of his, since they had come from the same place in Norway. One day while visiting Stromme, he said, "I have something to tell you, but I don't want you to tell anyone."

Stromme replied, "If I cannot tell it to my Ellen, you need not tell me." That was how fond he was of his wife. So the pastor had to tell him that he could tell Ellen that he was going to be married.

His bride came, I think, from the town of Scandinavia. I remember what snapping brown eyes she had. She was a short stout woman, very handsome, with brown hair parted in the middle and two long braids wound up around the back of her head. There was never a hair out of place. Her husband almost worshipped the ground she trod. They had six children or more in rapid succession —Karl, Clara, Willie, and so on. She was very quick with them and would apply the whip at the slightest provocation. One time she was trouncing one of them so hard that the pastor said gently,

"That's enough now, Mama," and the child was freed. They did not believe it was right to spare the rod and spoil the child in those days. As far as I know these children all grew up to be fine men and women, but certainly too much was expected of ministers' children then.

Homme was very glad to drink the simple homemade wines and beers in the homes of his congregation, but he was death on saloons and boughten drinks. One time one of his sons got a job in Butte des Morts in a store, for a short time. His father said after he had been there a while, "You don't ever go into the saloons in that wicked town, do you, my boy?"

He replied, "Why, Papa, what else is there to do in Butte des Morts?" You can be sure that Homme got him out of there in a hurry.

Homme was a very good friend of our family. He and Father loved each other dearly. Mother was always on hand with some special good wine that she had made for him, and called it *prestevin* (the preacher's wine). She also saved out the nicest-shaped cookies every time she baked to go with it. And if she had homemade beer, she would treat him with that, too. The ministers in those days thought nothing of taking a glass of beer. Not the drink, but the drunkenness was the sin. A couple of Lutheran ministers we knew would even go to a place in a near-by town where they sold groceries and beer both. They saw no harm in going in there and drinking a glass of beer while the grocer gathered up their order of groceries. Later on we found that it was a very common thing amongst the German Lutheran ministers in Oshkosh to drink beer even in saloons. Drinking beer was such a common everyday affair that it was taken for granted. The Biblical idea about being their brother's keeper, or leading someone astray by their example, never seems to have occurred to them. Only drunkenness was the disgrace.

Most of the early Norwegians were sick without their liquor. When they got to feeling low, both men and women, they would, if they could, get hold of some alcohol and sugar and water, with perhaps cinnamon for flavor, then they would immediately feel peppy and "run like a tailless cat," as the saying went. The Yankee

70

children in my childhood would taunt us Norwegians by flexing their knees and chanting,

> Ve get so dr-runk
> Ve don't know vat to do-oo,

imitating Tone's brother-in-law, who loved his bottle and his "vhisky." Drunkenness was fairly common in Norway until about 1850, I think. Then a strict licensing was introduced. They say now that many places in Norway have prohibition, and maybe they won't be noted for their drunkenness any more. But you could hardly blame them when even their ministers drank.

ONE TIME THERE was quite a disturbance amongst the whole congregation. They got to quarreling over Pastor Homme. There were several reasons for this quarrel, but it was mostly the fault of the people. For I am ashamed to tell you that the old Norwegians of that day were full of tricks. Not that they didn't possess some excellent virtues. They were good church members, believed absolutely in the Trinity and had hope of eternal life, shook in trembling at the thought of the Devil, and attended services faithfully. The women were particularly moral. Sometimes there was a hasty trip to the altar, of course. Sometimes an unfortunate girl would be left with her unnamed child. But after marriage all foolishness ended abruptly. The women of those days were absolutely faithful to their husbands, and coveted their good name above all things. I heard of only one instance where a married woman went wrong, and then it was only hearsay. Nobody ever witnessed it. She was a beautiful young girl who had been urged by her parents to marry a rich man, twenty years older. It was said that she carried on with someone else.

One other instance I can remember. At the parties which people were always having, some of the men got to feeling pretty good after so many glasses of liquor. There was a certain man who got to visiting with a likeable married woman at party after party. Finally one night when he was a little more tipsy than usual, he became even more chummy. He got up closer to her and said, "I *like* you, I *like* you," and named her name tenderly. She looked him right in the eye and calmly replied, "It's all right to like each other, but there's a limit to all things." And with that he was put in his place. "For better, for worse" meant just what it said in those days.

But both men and women were full of little sly tricks. The immigrants had so little to start out with that some of them thought up schemes to make a little extra money. They did not have too many cows, as they had to make their own butter and cheese. It was mostly in summer that they got anything out of their cows, and then the price of butter would be low because plenty was coming to market. So some of the women were shrewd enough not to sell butter until the fall. They all had good cold cellars with earthen floors, but even then, the butter would taste rancid after standing in jars down there all summer. So they would put a layer of fresh butter on the top of the jars, and wrap a nice clean cloth over the rim. The storekeeper who bought the butter would naturally take a small sample from the top, taking for granted that the whole jar was just like it. But they soon got onto the tricks and began to taste each jar with some kind of little spoon that went way to the bottom, and that put an end to that wickedness.

You can believe that my mother was above such crookedness. I don't know how long butter would have stayed sweet on our cellar floor, but it was surely clean. Every spring the old sand was swept off the hard earth, and new sand from our sand pit brought in to cover it. This naturally kept it from being musty. Our butter went to the market weekly.

One man added sweet buttermilk to the sweet milk he sold to the cheese factory, but he did not get away with that very long. Another fellow used to put stones in his hay load when he took it to market, but he, too, was caught. This same man tried a scheme to make his pigs weigh more when he took them to sell. He fed them so much salt that they drank an enormous quantity of water. But when he got to market they were almost ready to burst and he got caught at that, too. Pastor Homme tried to show people what a poor policy it was to be dishonest. No one got away with it very long, he said, and then your good name was gone forever. Of course it did not make the pastor popular to reprove sinners.

Another favorite trick the people did was to get hold of feeble, helpless old couples with property, tend them, make a fuss over them and then on the deathbed, hold the cold hand and make it trace a signature on a will, deeding everything to the seeming benefactor. Even if there was a will already made, some sly person would take in the old person and get him to deed all the property over. Sometimes one heir would beat all the other heirs out of their inheritance by putting in a terrible bill for care of the old folks, things they should have been glad to do for love alone. These things worried Pastor Homme when he heard of them, and he would try to make them right.

It must be said in the people's defense that Pastor Homme was not always tactful in correcting their sins. He looked like Martin Luther; he loved the very name of Martin Luther and tried to follow him in every way. And you know that Martin Luther was absolutely fearless in everything he said and did. He even talked to the Devil, and threw an ink bottle at him one day. Pastor Homme was like this. Sometimes he would try to make the sinner stand up in church and confess his sin and beg pardon. This often drove the sinner away from church for a long time, inflaming his family and friends, even though they knew he was in the wrong. Things went on, up and down for a while, but a climax had to come. It came about over a certain funeral sermon.

We were told that the pastor once went to the bedside of a dying man and asked him to confess his sins to God. The man replied, "I have never stolen, I have never killed anybody, and I have never committed adultery. I have nothing to confess." This frightened the pastor, and he pleaded that all men were sinners and that he must have something to confess so as to make peace with God. The dying man persisted that he was entirely innocent, and died without taking it back. At the funeral, it was said that Homme from his high pulpit, pointed to the casket sitting in front of the altar rail, and told in plain words what had taken place at the bedside. Now, it was customary at a funeral to praise the deceased for his Christian virtues, if any, at least to make the best of things, but certainly not to condemn him. After this sermon, people were roused in their wrath and wanted to put the pastor out then and there. Others were just as strong for him, and the quarrel kept on.

Another thing that made trouble was that Homme tried to make the young people stop their awful drinking and dancing. People held public dances in their homes. Not a week went by in winter without one somewhere, and they were well attended. The host did not charge any admission, but a collection was always taken up for the fiddler, at least a dollar and a half, or two. We were told that one time Homme passed a house at night, all lit up and full of people, and stopped his horse in the road to see what they were doing. What he saw was the subject of many and many a sermon and of a pamphlet, distributed widely, for Pastor Homme was a fearless man and spoke and wrote what he thought. He felt it not unreasonable to ask that a congregation which professed such love for Christianity be a little different from worldly ones. He kept harping on this subject of dancing and drinking so much that the young people got down on him.

Well, sides began to form in the fight, and it went so far that those that were against him pulled out of the congregation. This great break was called the *splittelse*. Thirty-five members and their families left and formed their own congregation. This happened in 1870. These people built a church of their own, right beside the old one, just a few rods away. They could even hear each other singing. A minister of their own was obtained, and they had to rent a house a mile from the church for him to live in, since the old parsonage naturally belonged to the old church. They even put a fence right down the middle of the old churchyard, so that funerals could be held separately. Well, you can imagine the jealousy, the slams, the slurs that went on between the two congregations. For instance, the ceiling of the new church was painted with gold stars. The naughty boys of the old church would say, "Oh, those swell people! Even the stars shine in the daytime for them!" I was just a young girl then. Our folks stayed, but my future husband's family (Tone's) were among those that left. It was a sin and a shame the way they acted.

The *splittelse* made a lot of trouble for everyone. For instance, when there were weddings, if one of the couple belonged to the old church, and the other to the new, each wanted to be married in his or her own church. It usually ended up with the groom giving in. When I got married, my husband's folks were still so bitter against our dear old Pastor Homme that I knew they would have a fit if I mentioned the old church, even though he had left four years before. They still would not set foot inside the old church except for funerals or a wedding of some relative. After our marriage I went with my husband to the new church, and there was no trouble between us on that subject. It all sounded so foolish to me.

Pastor Homme moved away from Winchester after having served the congregation there for fourteen years, and they must have been sad ones for him. I was one of the last confirmation class he had in Winchester. He then started a home for the aged and orphans in Wittenberg, Wisconsin; it was called the Homme Home. There was nothing but wild woods where he built it, and many a hard day did he put in before he got it started and on its feet. He did not live to be very old, only about seventy. In his last days, I have been told, he prayed to the Lord that he might get a place, if only a small place, inside of the Heavenly Door. If he did not get inside of the door of Heaven, I don't know how it will be for the rest of us. I never saw him again after he left Winchester, but I never forgot him, nor did I forget his good teachings and the advice that he gave us while we took instructions from him before confirmation. He gave us each a little note book in which he had us write down some special hymns. I still have that little book and still, at the age of eighty-three read those beautiful hymns over and over.

AFTER A PERIOD of twenty-three years, the two congregations began to come together again. The first step was to have only one minister serve both congregations. Finally they agreed to tear down the two old churches and build a new one on the site of the first one. Now they outdid themselves in making the new one beautiful, as if to wipe out the bad feelings and make it acceptable to God after all their sinning. My husband and his stepfather and a man named John Uvaas were three of the main helpers. My John was a very skilled carpenter. I have been told that he and his stepfather built the *predikestol*, communion rail, and altar. He and I gave a big stained-glass window by the pulpit, and our names are on it in gold letters. My husband's uncle, Captain Ole Oleson, gave the two handsome windows on each side of the altar at the back of the new chancel.

In that old church you seldom hear a Norwegian word now. Even the name is changed. Instead of the United Lutheran Church, it is Grace Lutheran Church, which seems strange to us older ones to whom the word United meant so much. And there is not one Norwegian sermon any more. Many of the congregation would not understand it, even though they are descendants of the early members. They keep the church in excellent repair; it is really a beautiful place. And instead of the unschooled farmers, there are now ministers, music teachers, schoolteachers, nurses; and every child may have at least a high-school education. The farmers have all kinds of machinery to do their hard work, but help is not as plentiful as in the old days; these educated people don't want to work on farms.

When John and I were approaching our golden wedding, the old friends wrote to us and tried to have us celebrate it in that church, for all the work John did on it, and our long connection with it on both sides of the family. But we had been away from the community so long that we felt it better to have it at our farm at Waupaca. All the old friends came up there to celebrate with us, and I will tell you about it in the last chapter.

Our children have always been proud to go to that old church and see the work their father did, and the windows with our family names on them. It is something nice for them to feel that their family has been connected with one church in this new land for a hundred years.

CHILDHOOD

IN MY CHILDHOOD home I never knew what worry or trouble was. I was a strong, healthy child and loved to help my parents with everything I could possibly do, both indoors and out. I could milk cows, feed calves, and work in the fields like a man, although Father saw to it that a girl never did any heavy lifting or labor. There were so many light tasks on the farm those days, such as raking, hoeing, tying bundles of grain, picking up vegetables and fruit, that children were kept busy at all times.

The strange thing was that I never seemed to get tired. I could be at dances and parties when I got older, I am almost ashamed to tell it, until two or three o'clock in the morning, and we would not only walk over, but back, several miles. When we got home there would only be time for a couple of hours sleep, and I would be fit for a whole day's work, if it was at a busy time of the year.

I look back on that happy childhood home as a paradise. We had such a lovely big lawn at the old home. From the front door we had a path going to the road, with a long flower bed on each side of it. At each end of these flower beds we had some kind of shrubs or trees, lilacs or snowball bushes. Near by were plum trees. Here and there were round flower beds. When these all blossomed in the spring, the fragrance and beauty were wonderful to experience. West of the house was like an outdoor living room.

At the west edge of the lawn grew a row of plum trees. On the south of these and back again towards the house were crab-apple and apple trees and more plums. Oh, how good these tasted to our thirsty mouths in summer! Just one bite would puncture the skin of those little red plums, and our mouths would be full of sweet cool juice.

Near the west door of the new kitchen was a big oak tree. We had planted chives all around the base of it, and it was one of our pleasures to go out there with thick slices of Mother's bread and butter, and make sandwiches of those chives.

The greatest tree on the place was a hickory that grew a little distance from the southeast of the house. The nuts on this tree had very thin shells, and the meats were rich and full. It was a dandy tree. Beneath it was a huge granite boulder with a flat top where we would sit and crack those nuts in the fall. The trees of childhood have a tendency to get bigger and bigger in the memory. But I believe this tree was just as tall and wide as I remembered it, because we have a picture of the farm yard, taken when I was grown, and that hickory tree simply dwarfs the log house and everything around it. It is still standing but I believe it has broken off some.

A little way from the house stood a small building we called the cook shanty. It had just three walls and a slanting roof; the front was all open. Inside were an old cook stove and a long bench to set ourselves and the waterpail on. A few shelves along the back part of it held the pans and kettles. There was just an earthen floor which we kept swept clean with a broom. Oh dear, how many good meals my mother cooked in that shanty! The new potatoes and sweet corn! Good salt pork was about the only kind of meat we had through the summer, and we never got tired of it fried, with milk gravy made from the drippings. I could never tire of eating the crispy meat, and chewing the brittle, browned rind. Often we had corned beef. On Sunday we would have chicken sometimes, with lots of gravy and fluffy yellow dumplings.

By fall the salt pork would be used up, too, and then we would kill a sheep or two. We had smoked hams and bacon once in a while, but not until we were older. The farmers seemed to prefer the salted meat in the early days.

Those were the happy carefree days, and I know the people were happier than they are now. We didn't have to worry about keeping up with the Joneses, for we were all about alike, though some had more money than others. We didn't have to worry about wars and depressions. People were happy over very little. The neighbors had time to visit each other and give parties. Some of my children have lived next door to the same neighbors for years and don't even know them. That would have been impossible in my day.

My father, whose job it was to scrub the new potatoes for Mother, fixed up some sort of brush to skin them, and it would not be hard for anyone to do the same today. It was made as they had made them in Norway, of a lot of twigs from a certain stout bush, which were tied securely around a broom handle, and the brush cut off even. The potatoes were put in a pail and covered with water and then stomped with the brush until the skins were all off. When he would pour this water off and rinse the potatoes, they were smooth and shining, ready to cook. I can see my father now, stomping those potatoes, outside the little cook shanty. Father always brought in the vegetables and killed the chickens. He loved my mother so that it was a pleasure to help her in any way.

In those days the only tame berries we had were currants, but there were all kinds of wild red raspberries and blackcaps and black-berries and strawberries. We found them along fences. At the end of our farm was a marsh, and along the south side of it, where the land was low, there were masses of these bushes. The pails of raspberries I picked there I could not remember now, but I know there were a good many of them each season. On the other side of this marsh were strawberries. Wild strawberries were not so very big, but so sweet and good. Oh, how we loved to pick and eat these berries! I was married and gone from home before my parents got some tame strawberry plants from Halvor and Anne Johnson and started a bed near the house. These were among the first tame ones to come to our township.

Hazelnut bushes grew thick along the zig-zag rail fences and all over the woods on that long hill on our farm. We used to pick them in gunny sacks and had to be careful to watch very closely for some nasty long insects called Devil Horses. They used to hang on these bushes, and looked just like long green sticks with four lanky legs. They were said to be poisonous if they bit you, but we never gave them a chance to prove it.

We would haul these hazelnuts home and lay them on top of the roof of the cook shanty. It was so low on the back end that we could easily get up there by standing on a barrel or something. We emptied our bags of hazelnuts on the roof and let them lie there in the sun until they were dry enough to shuck. Then, how we cracked and ate them! We used to find a stone that had a little hollow place, and lay them in there and crack them with a hammer.

Then came hickory-nut time. Picking was my job, if we had to climb the trees to get them. There were hickory trees all over

81

the farm. There was one great, tall tree on the side of the big hill whose branches were high from the ground. But the nuts were as large as small crab apples, and if we did not get them the squirrels would. When I got old enough to worry about it, I stood under that tree one day and looked longingly at those big nuts, wondering how in the world I could get at them. They were even too high from the ground to reach with a long stick. So I said to myself, I am going to see if I can climb that tree. I took a long stick in one hand (it seems impossible now) and grasped the trunk with both hands, hitching myself up that tree like a monkey, and finally reached the lowest branch. From then on it was easy, for I could climb from branch to branch and hit the nuts off with the long stick. I tell you I was proud to be the first person to conquer that tree, but the nuts were worth it. If I had not been born with that determination and strength, I guess I would have been dead long ago. My lifetime motto has been, "Never get stuck."

These nuts would have been eaten up by our big family quicker than the squirrels had it not been for quick-thinking brother John. He laid them on boards across the upstairs rafters in the house, where they had a fine place to dry. A few at the time would be brought down and put in a round tin box which was kept under the kitchen lounge. Very nice cakes would be decorated or filled with these delicious nut meats, and many were the long evenings when the wind and snow were whirling outside, that we children sat on the couch and cracked and ate the good nuts.

There were many wild grape vines around the farm, too, in those days. We children had to go after the grapes with baskets, and we had to be careful not to crush them. My mother made wine, as was the style everywhere, and treated the friends who came to see us. This is what the grapes were used for. Sometimes she made wine out of currants. That was really delicious.

For these outings, you can believe, we wore our most raggedy clothes. By the time we came back they would be torn with briers and bark, and stained with grass and berry juice. Then the next washday we would be invited to help wash them. I began my washing career standing on a box so that I could reach the washboard in the tub.

Mother washed by the old cook shanty, where it was handy to the stove for heating water and boiling clothes, and where there was plenty of shade in the morning. The clothesline was near by. We caught rain water in barrels that stood beside the house, but if it was low because of a dry spell, we would rinse the clothes in water from the pump.

We had a sort of washing machine, too, a kind that was common amongst our people. The clothes were put into a smooth, small barrel with warm water and our good, soft, homemade soap. They were then stomped with a stomper which Father had made. Its head was a solid piece of smooth, hard wood, with two cutouts scooped out of the bottom, but not all the way through. On top of this head he bored a hole into which he inserted a long handle. I suppose these cutouts helped to get the dirt out of the clothes by suction. We had to stomp them only a few minutes, wring them out, put them in another clean suds in the tub to rub stubborn spots on the board, such as edges of cuffs and collars, and then rinse them in clean water. Believe me, the clothes were clean after this second scrubbing and rinsing. The final water was the bluing, then starching, if needed, and out on the clothesline they would go, to blow and dry in the wind and sun. Think of it! Some of those clothes were wrung out by hand five times, and we never seemed to mind it. We didn't know there was, or would be, any other way to wash clothes. Mechanical wringers were unheard of.

For blankets and quilts this barrel washing could not be beat. The wool blankets were as light and clean and fluffy as they could be when they were rinsed and dried. If the rain barrels got entirely empty, then we had to wash with well water softened with ashes the day before. One had to use good judgment not to use too many, however, or the water would be too hard on the clothes as well as on our hands.

Our soap was made out of clarified fat drippings, or lard, and lye. Toward the spring of the year, Mother had Father get her a big barrel. He set this on two blocks high enough from the ground so that a fairly good-sized trough made of wood could stand a little way under the barrel. Then every day they would empty the ashes from the stove into the barrel. It had to be ashes from hard wood. When the barrel was full, water was poured over the ashes until they were soaked. Then the lye would begin to seep through the barrel and run into the trough. They had to watch so that the lye would not run over. There was a large iron kettle into which they emptied the lye.

In the meantime they had to pour more water over the ashes until they had all the lye they wanted. Then they put the lye over the outdoor fireplace. Now into this would go a lot of soap fat that had been saved from the time they had butchered their hogs in the fall. When they had their big family at home, they would have butchered four or five hogs and a beef animal and put the meat up for the winter. Mother had also saved all the scrap fat that accumulated through the winter. Now she boiled this fat and lye until all the grease was gone, then she let it stand until the next day, at which time she added soft water. There was a dasher attached to a broom handle with which she churned the soap and kept adding water until it was smooth and brown and jelly-like. When it was cool, it was stored in a barrel in the cellar. This soap was soap! You never saw nicer suds. It was not perfumed, but it did not smell bad, and it did not skin your hands.

Soap could be made of tallow, too. Mother usually used five pounds of melted tallow to one can of Lewis lye. She melted the tallow to lukewarm, poured in the lye, and stirred it slowly with a flat, wooden stick until it was of the consistency of honey. This soap was poured into a wooden box lined with an old piece of cloth. It was covered and kept in a warm place until the next day. By that time it would be hard enough to cut into bars, and it was very good soap. Sometimes this soap was perfumed in the making.

AFTER THE crops were in each fall, we children were allowed to go to school. The little white frame schoolhouse had a small entry where we hung our wraps. The rest was one big room for studying and reciting lessons: a long row of seats close to the wall on each side, with a space in front for recitations. Half of one wall was of blackboards, where problems were worked under the teacher's eye. In front were her desk and some seats where naughty ones had to sit and study.

Just in from these outside seats there was an aisle, and then another row of double seats on each side of the room. The middle of the room was empty save for a big stove. In this space the teacher went up and down to help us with problems we did not understand. If someone needed help, he raised his hand. Some would have the nerve to snap their fingers, if she did not notice them quickly enough. Our teachers were mostly Yankee old maids, very refined and pleasant, but one time we did have a married woman, our neighbor, Amy Hough. The teachers were very gentle with the girls and with all children who minded, but unruly boys had to be called to the front, made to hold out their hands and get them smacked with a ruler every now and then. This used to make me feel terrible, for I could never stand trouble. When I grew up and had eight children, I could hardly ever bear to switch them.

The teachers wore mostly long worsted dresses with high collars and long sleeves. Short sleeves were just not worn in those days. And no nice woman ever parted her hair on the side. Our teachers either parted theirs in the middle, or combed it straight back, with a braid wound around in the back or on top of the head. Everybody wore high-top laced or buttoned shoes to school, and almost everywhere. I was eighteen years old when I had my first pair of slippers. They were black patent leather with rounded toes and medium heels. They were laced with sky-blue laces which had fluffy tassels at the end. I remember how embarrassed I was at a picnic once when a young man knelt and pulled at one of those tassels and said, "Well, what is this?"

One time we had a teacher who came with the new idea that children needed exercise. We, who worked and played from morning till night! But she meant exercise to music. While she played the organ, we put arms up, arms down, arms in, arms out. The big boys felt foolish doing it, but the rest of us liked it.

There were many spelling-downs. One time in our school house there were about forty spellers lined up on both sides of the room. As I was a good speller, I was trying to stand up the longest. Just the next to the last one, I went down on a word I'll never forget. It was "mackerel," and I spelled it "mackeral." I think I was about thirteen years old at the time.

Spelling-downs were such a lot of fun that the room would be full of people listening. Some of them would join in. One time Hans Jorgensen got up to spell. He was the one that Mother thought was an Indian climbing into our window one night. I never will forget how everybody laughed when his time came to spell. He was given the word "chair" and he said solemnly, "c–h–a–r." The whole schoolhouse rocked with laughter. We had so much fun to see how the different words were spelled. There do not seem to be so many innocent ways of having fun these days. We walked to these spelling-downs, too, a mile over and a mile back.

When I got to be about ten or eleven years old, I had to take over the family letter-writing. Two of my older sisters, Hattie and Anguline, married only two months apart and moved about two hundred miles away. There was no one to write to them since my parents had never learned how. Brother Ole could have, but like all men, he hated writing letters. So it was up to me.

One letter my parents got was from a young man asking for the hand of another beloved sister, Sena, who was away from home at the time. I did not think I could answer a letter like that, but my parents dictated it, and so I wrote, giving their consent. It was written in Norwegian. I guess I was about sixteen or seventeen years old at the time. In reply, I got a little present from the young man for answering this important letter to him. He sent me a lovely red and white beaded basket, with a beaded cover and handle and even a beaded clasp. Inside was a large silk handkerchief of red, with a border of yellow, blue, and green stripes around the edge. I did not use it for a few years until girls began to wear such nice handkerchiefs around their necks under their coats.

I am sorry to say that my sister Sena turned this young man down and went back to a very stylish, handsome man whose company she had kept some time before. She felt so sorry for the man she turned down that she gave him my picture and told him that I was as like her as could be in all ways, and that perhaps he could win me. He began to write to me, and the letters became very loving. I answered the first one, and then I began to think: "Now, what do I want with answering letters to this old man. Here I am only sixteen, and he is at least twenty-six." So I quit writing, and then he had to. But I kept that nice basket. After John and I were married, I hung it on the fancy top of my dresser, over the looking glass. Somehow John found out who gave it to me, and he was so jealous that he could never bear to look at it. One time when we moved, it turned up missing, and you know the person I suspected.

I had also to read all the letters we got from the relatives in Norway. My parents could read printing, but could not write script nor read it. The majority of country children in Norway studied only religion in school, and my parents were great readers. But neither of them could even sign their names and had to use an X. I am surprised that my father's three schoolmaster brothers never taught him to write. I had to be very careful when my parents dictated letters for me to write in Norwegian to these learned men. Of course, I had learned to write and spell Norwegian in parochial school.

A great many of the country children did not even finish the English country school—not amongst the Norwegians, though some of the Yankees might have. Oh, some of those blue-belly Yankees were mean to us! They used to make fun of us when we first started school because we talked English so brokenly. But you should have heard them when they tried to talk Norwegian. That was even funnier. We Norwegians soon learned the English language perfectly, and could then speak in two tongues. The Yankees could speak only one, so they had nothing on us after a few years. The sad part about those early days was that many Norwegian children did not get to go to English school at all and were handicapped all their lives. My two younger sisters and I went, and the two children next older, Anne and brother John, went for a little while. The oldest children could go only a few weeks in winter, for all the rest of the time they had to work, either at home or somewhere else.

I NEVER GOT a full term of school myself. In the fall we had to help with the corn husking, potato digging, and getting the garden stuff in. I would lose at least a month or six weeks each fall. Then

I could attend school regularly until the grass got long enough in the spring for the cows to graze. Since not all the fields were fenced in, the cows had to be watched from early morning until about ten or eleven o'clock, when they had their fill. If we did not watch them, they would wander over into the fields of newly-sown oats.

My two little sisters, Lena and Kristine, went along for company. Lena could not run after the cows when they got unruly, because of her lame leg. Kristine was too little, so it all fell to me and the dog. Our Fido was a black, smooth-haired dog, with brown spots over his eyes. He was a good cow dog, and would stay with us a while, but soon there was no dog in sight. Presently we would hear a barking up in the woods, and know that he had gone after more exciting adventure, such as chasing rabbits, chipmunks, and squirrels.

When the cows got a little satisfied in some thick grass, there was nothing to do for us, either. So we would have to look around for something to entertain ourselves. We would make playhouses in the woods and have all the fun in the world. Rooms were partitioned off with branches broken from young trees or hazelnut bushes. Flat stones were our chairs and tables. I remember one very large flat stone in particular that was the organ. You should have seen and heard us singing and playing on that organ. We thoroughly enjoyed the concerts we gave ourselves. Then we would give parties for each other in our respective houses. Near the time to go home, we would pick pinkish-white lady slippers, called in Norwegian *Jomfru Maria sko* (Virgin Mary slipper). There was wild purple phlox and another sort of white flower with a yellow center whose petals hung down. Yellow cowslips grew along the stream in the spring, and banks of purple violets, and later on black-eyed Susans and lots of wild pink roses. Mother was very fond of flowers and was always pleased when we brought her some.

About ten or eleven o'clock in the morning, the cows would be full and start slowly for home in a pretty, long line. At home they would get water and then the rest of the day they stayed in the fenced pasture. In those days we had only six or seven cows and a few young calves to tend, and it wasn't hard. We always looked forward to the spring when we could get out in the lovely woods and watch the cows.

In the wintertime when we were little, Mother never required anything of us but washing dishes, and so we had time for another sort of fun. After school and on Saturdays, we spent hours sliding on the ice with our shoes. No one had skates then, which will surprise you, since we came from Norway. I don't think they had skates over there, either. We slid on a pond below the barn. Father had a big sled upon which he used to haul wood from the woodshed to the house. This he let us use to slide down steep hills. There was room for all of us to sit on it. The first trip down wouldn't go as well as the following ones, after a track had been made for the sledrunners. They were made of hard wood and were as slippery as glass, and we could go lickety-split down the longer hills.

All Norwegians went on skis. It was wonderful fun to stand up and slide down hill on them. I could even stand on one alone with both feet and slide down without falling, going as fast as on two skis. I guess I was the only one of our bunch that could do that. I stuck to it just as I did trying to climb that great hickory tree; finally I learned how.

The neighborhood children joined us in these sports, and there was quite a crowd of us at times. One time one of the neighbor boys took a notion to train a couple of yearling steers to haul us on one bob of the big sleigh. He hitched them to this bob some way. After we all got seated safely on the bob, the steers went pretty well for a while, then they balked. They would not run so very long before they slowed down to a dull walk and stubbornly headed for home. We enjoyed these rides while they lasted.

EACH SUMMER we had a few weeks of parochial school, which was always conducted by a man. Some of these teachers later studied to be ministers. We were all compelled to go, all the children, that is. The sole purpose of this school was to teach religion; it also gave the Norwegian children a chance to learn their parents' mother tongue. They began going at the age of six, and continued until they were confirmed. The session lasted nine weeks, five days a week, every summer. Since the congregation was divided into three districts for this purpose, no child could give the excuse that he lived too far away, for the three schools ran at the same time in different districts. All of our teachers were Norwegian men, of course. One teacher I remember was Jorgen Madson. He taught us many nice songs, but I cannot remember even the first lines of them, I am sorry to say.

The first thing in the morning, we would have a prayer then a religious song. The classes were long and lasted until noon, when we were loosed for a wonderful hour of lunch and fun. At the Mathison schoolhouse (English school in winter) we had make-believe playhouses in which we played at noon. Each party had a big tree that was theirs, and we would visit each other like grown-ups. It never got tiresome. All too soon the bell would ring, and we would have to go back inside and study again. We knew the day was at an end when the teacher told us to put away our books for the closing prayer and song.

I can remember some of the things we studied at parochial school: first reader A-B-C for the little ones, *lesebok* (reader) for the older ones, Bible history, New Testament, *catechismus, for-klaring* (explanation of the five parts in the catechism), and singing.

During the weeks that we were in parochial school, Mother had to watch the cows at their morning pasture. Part of the time this would be in the grain field after the grain had been hauled off. Mother loved this chore. She would take her dog along and a religious book, and I am sure that this walk out in the sunshine was a relief from all the hard work she had to do. She could sit and rest and read while they were feeding. After about three hours or so, the cows would be satisfied and ready to start in a long line for home, with Fido yapping at their heels.

I WAS ALWAYS very fond of music, and we had a lot of it at home. Brother Ole played the violin, and Father sang hymns in the morning every day of his life. Even when he was over ninety years old, he taught my children to sing hymns. I can always remember hearing him sing as I woke in the morning. It left a much nicer memory than the modern radio or alarm clock. In English school we learned many songs, "Grandfather's Clock," "In the Sweet By and By," "Rock of Ages," "Jesus, Lover of My Soul," "Old Oaken Bucket," "Home, Sweet Home," and many others.

The only musical instruments the farmers around us had in those early days were fiddles. Little by little as they got ahead and in better circumstances, some of them would buy reed organs. A music teacher from a near-by town would drive around the country with a horse and top buggy once a week and give lessons to anyone who wanted them. The lessons were not more than twenty-five or thirty-five cents apiece. It was a great thing when a girl got so far in music that she could play church hymns and a funeral and a wedding march. If they got to the place where they could play the bigger reed organ in the church, they were considered good musicians, and their folks would nearly burst with pride.

Brother Ole was the chief fiddler in our town, as they called them in that time. He had an American violin then, but later a Hardanger violin that was brought from Norway, which he played until he got deaf in his late eighties. It was all inlaid with mother-of-pearl and at the end there was a gilded head like on the prow of a Viking ship. This violin had two banks of strings, the upper one for playing, and the lower for resonance. He played by ear, but the music was there. With that good ear for music and his nimble fingers, it seemed that the dancers had no trouble dancing after his fiddling. Whenever there was a dance or a wedding, Ole had to come with his fiddle, and did they ever dance and have fun!

My mother never liked the idea of his playing like that, for there was usually drinking, especially for the fiddler. He had to get enough in him to put life in that fiddle. So she was very glad when another man named Sam Traar and his brother, Thomas, took the lead in fiddling. They really had my brother beat, because one played first violin and the other second. Sam was a real musician. He had taken lessons and became the best fiddler in the entire country. When Sam Traar played, we got very light on our feet. He could play any dance music there was, "Turkey in the Straw," "Old Washerwoman," or anything. He played with such fire that his head and feet and everything kept time.

We were almost beside ourselves with joy and pride when Halvor, Hattie's husband, brought Mother the little yellow hand organ and put it in the big room of the old log house. It was about a foot and a half long, a foot wide and a foot high, of yellow wood with red roses painted on it. In the back was a sort of bellows, and at the front a lot of little metal clappers that fitted over small holes. Below these clappers was a place for the roller to fit in. The rollers were fitted in various music patterns with fine nails whose heads had been taken off. As the handle at the side was turned, it pumped up the bellows at the back, and at the same time turned the roller. These long nails hit the tails of the clappers, lifting them off the holes, and letting the music out. It was fascinating for us children to see Mother play that organ. Many fine pieces came with the machine. A favorite one was *Farvel, Du Gamle Norge* (Farewell, Old Norway), and the words went like this:

> Farewell, old Norway
> No more shall I see thee
> So shall you have full many thanks
> For all you've done for me....

I can see Mother now, winding up that old organ and listening to the music, while the tears ran down her cheeks. She took so much comfort with it, even though it did make her cry.

FOR A SIMPLE country home, I believe ours was one with a good deal of refinement. It was natural for Mother and Father, and we learned it directly and indirectly from them. They were great on "respect," and we heard it morning, noon, and night. They were forever preaching to us to be modest and nice-behaving. When we were sent to a neighbor on an errand, especially to some that were kind of inquisitive, we were warned not to tell a thing about affairs at home. Just say, "I don't know." They were very particular about this, as they did not want anyone to know about their business, and they were right. It doesn't pay to tell everybody everything one knows.

Never must we act like we were wild, at a party or any place, but should be nice and quiet wherever we were. When it came time to have beaus come to see us, if Mother ever caught us sitting so close to any man that we touched, she would give us a terrible talking-to after he had left. It was considered disrespectable in her eyes for us to touch a man, except to hold his hand in dancing, or to have him whirl us around in a dance, which he had to do. Even married women lost standing in her sight if they touched their men in front of people. She considered it coarse and common.

Oh, deary me, how times have changed
Since Grandma was a girl....

I never could see though, that it was right to hold children down too hard. John and I never objected to our children having all the fun they possibly could. He used to say as they left the house, "Have all the fun you want, but don't get gay."

IN MY CHILDHOOD I was never sick, except for a few diseases that swept the country. One time the smallpox was very bad. Some of our family got it. I was only five years old then, and had it so bad that my face was one solid scab. Mother told me not to pick it, or it would leave a deep hole, and luckily I had sense enough to obey her, for I have not one scar left from that terrible experience. We all got over it but a young cousin, Andres, the oldest child of Uncle Ole Böe and Aunt Aslaug. He had what was called the black smallpox and died at the age of nineteen. It was a terrible thing for those poor parents to lose that boy; he was so unusually kind and promising.

We didn't have a doctor when we had the smallpox, or for another time when we three youngest ones took the measles. Mother just put us in a dark room, as it was known even then that light in the eyes during that disease would make one have weak sight.

One time Kristine got a bad bladder trouble. It was so awful that our folks did call a doctor, and she got over it all right. But she was never strong. Mother had two sorrows from what sicknesses we did have as children. When Lena was a year and a half old, she got what they thought was a boil on the hip. It hurt her

93

so to walk that she began to sit on the floor, with the hurt leg bent backwards at the knee. No doctor was called for this ailment. Everybody thought she'd get over it. It was a long time before she finally got up to walk again, and then the tendon at the back of the sore leg was drawn up, making it shorter than the other. So Lena was lame from that day forward. This hurt Mother so much that she could never get over it. She would never let anyone be cross to Lena in any way, and did everything she could all the rest of her life to make up for that deformity.

When Kristine was eleven years old, she and Lena took the dreadful disease, diphtheria, for which there was then no prevention and no cure. They called a doctor from Winneconne this time, but he said he could do nothing. Kristine died. This was a frightful blow to all of us, for she was as much like an angel as a person could be, and we had had such a lovely childhood together. But it was God's will that she should go. It was my father's peculiarity that he had never shed tears, but when this happened, tears rolled down his cheeks.

It was in summer when she died. Everybody was so terrified over the dreadful disease that they did not even dare to take her into the church for the funeral, but held it in the churchyard by the open grave. Only a few brave friends and relatives came, and even they stood afar off, with handkerchiefs to their mouths. We had a man in our pastorate then whose name was Omlid. He was a young man with long waving silken sideburns that hung over his stiff white ruff. His eyes were as mild and tender as a woman's, and the congregation loved him. He did not fear to go near the casket, where Mother and Father and Sister Sena and I were weeping. None of the rest of the family could come, because Lena was still very sick at home. I can still remember one thing that Pastor Omlid said that day. Indicating us with his hand, he said: "You might as well ask a stream to stop flowing, as to ask these mourners to dry their tears."

MY CHILDHOOD ended, you might say, with confirmation in the Norwegian Lutheran church at Winchester. After that I did not go much more to the English school, either. I had finished almost through the fifth reader and had studied geography, arithmetic, spelling, reading, and writing; and I had already much more education than anyone in the family, or most of the girls of our acquaintance. The only subject I had not studied in our school was Constitution, and I don't know much about it to this day. So it was time to quit. My parents let me finish out that last year after I was confirmed, but one was supposed to be pretty much through school after confirmation.

I was fourteen when I started to take instructions. It was the year before Kristine died, and it was Pastor Homme's last confirmation class. We went to recite our lessons to him every Saturday for a year. These meetings were held in the sacristy back of the altar in our church. Pastor Homme was a good teacher, as well as our beloved minister.

There were five subjects to study: Bible history, Hymnal, New Testament, Catechism, and Explanation of the Catechism. The last two of these books we were supposed to learn by heart, and the hymns we wrote down in a little notebook that he gave us. We went from November to November. By the time we were to be confirmed, there was not one question or not even a word in that Catechism and the Explanation that I did not know by heart and could not answer. But it meant a lot of hard work. I used to go by myself away from everybody to study the lessons. When it came to the Explanation, there were first questions, then answers below them. I had the Catechism with me, and would lay it over the answers so that I could not see them, ask myself the questions, and answer them. The questions I got stuck on I would study until I knew them perfectly.

In this sacristy where the class met were two long tables, one on each side of the room, one for the boys and one for the girls. Besides me, only one of these girls is still living—Lena Dahlstrom Stimes. There were some boys in our class that just could not learn, and maybe did not try too hard. Anyway, our poor pastor was very much disappointed in them. One day while he was rehearsing the lessons with the boys, he noticed two of them looking down whenever they were to answer. The pastor soon found out why. Every time he asked them a question, they read the answers out of books in their laps. Pastor Homme was too smart not to catch on. He closed his book and hit first one then the other on the side of the head until their ears got red. We all got cold all over and scared to pieces. I guess those boys never tried such a trick again. It was bad enough to cheat in school, but to cheat in the church was too much. Some boys had to go two years instead of one before they learned their books well enough to stand the examination.

Then the great day came for the confirmation. Everybody had a new outfit from top to toe. I had a plum-colored dress with cuffs and a stand-up collar of lavender satin. It had a tight basque waist and a full skirt that came to the tops of the new high-top, black, buttoned shoes. I wore a grey felt hat, turned up all the way around except in the back, where the ribbon bow was. I had a new black wool coat, too, and black wool gloves. My dear big sister Sena was with me to help buy the outfit. She made the coat and dress, which assured me that it would not only be the latest style but very well done. She was almost perfect in all ways, and we were very close to each other.

I was so ashamed of the color of my hair that I thought it spoiled the whole outfit. Why couldn't I have been born with black hair like my parents, or beautiful blonde like Kristine or Lena? No, it was auburn, like my father's mother, Ingrid Haevre. Red hair was such a disgrace in those days that people teased me for a "redhead." There was so much of it that it could not be hidden—I could sit on the two long thick braids. Right around this time my brother and I had been out with the horse and cutter and happened to drive past Tone's place. That boy of hers, John, came out to talk to us. He told me years afterward that he was tempted almost beyond his strength that day to cut off one of those braids. He was always so proud of my hair.

The day we were confirmed we were placed in rank as the pastor ordered us. Oh, how I wanted to be first! I think I was the only one who knew the two books by heart. But, for various personal reasons, he put two other girls ahead of me, and I loved him too much to resent it. He lined us up in the aisle of the church, boys on one side, girls on the other, and walked up and down between us, asking questions. It was a great ordeal for us all. From where I stood, I could see Father's tender gaze, and could feel Mother's eyes boring a hole in my back. I wouldn't have shamed them for the world.

After the examination, we followed the pastor to the altar. He went inside the rail, and we knelt around it. Starting at the head, he asked us one by one in a solemn voice, "Will you renounce the Devil and all his works, believe that Christ died for your sins, and stand firm in this faith until the end of your days?" We replied, "I do." He then concluded, "Give me your hand, and God your heart," and shook hands with each of us. In his confirmation sermon he stressed the importance of the Christian life, and asked us earnestly to abide by our promise. It was all such a strain that we were happy when it was over, and we could get outside the church and take a deep breath. The next Sunday we took our first communion at that same altar rail, and from then on, we were members of the church.

I am sorry to say that very few of us kept the entire promise, or heeded our dear pastor's pleadings on that day. He was still against dances, but it was not more than a year before we began to go to them. If it was the Devil's work, as he said, we could not see it that way. It was his argument that dancing so close aroused evil passions. Maybe they danced like that in some places, but we did not. Ours was just clean, innocent fun, the most real gay fun I ever had in my life. If it was a sin, then I am sorry.

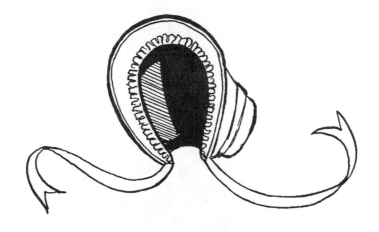

NEIGHBORS

IT IS HARD TO beat the Scandinavians for hospitality. Not only did the young folks have parties, but the old folks, too. They used any old excuse for a party. When there was work attached, it was called a bee, and there were many of these—plowing bees, husking bees, quilting bees. After these affairs, in the evening, the young folks would dance and have a big time. Of course, it was not a right good time until they had had a few drinks. Just enough to make them feel good, as they worded it, but with some it would be a little more. The newcomers were the ones who had the biggest time of all. They were so very lonesome for the old homeland, that when they could get together with friends from their same town in Norway, they were almost beside themselves with joy. It took them years to get used to the new style in America, and this group of old friends from home was their salvation.

One of the last of our folks to come over was John Böe, a great-nephew of Mother's. He made his home with us for quite a while, and how they pumped him about everything over in the old country. He taught parochial school for some time, then got a job in a small village store about nine miles away. The Norwegians, when asked where John Böe was, would reply, *"Han staar paa store i Butte des Morts."* Translated literally this is: "He stands on a store in Butte des Morts." This phrase used to amuse us children a great deal, because someone of our friends was always "standing on a store" some place. After the proprietor of the store died, John Böe became the owner, and he is still there. He helped refresh my memory about Gaarden Böe.

After a number of years, when brother Ole had taken over the farm, my folks felt that they could put up a good barn. Some of the material for it was sawed out of logs from our own swamp, and when all things were gathered, they had a barn-raising bee. It was in the springtime before the men had to go out on the fields.

Every neighbor for miles around was invited. And believe me, there was food prepared for such a crowd, and the women all helped prepare it. They had killed a calf for the occasion. Hundreds of doughnuts, cookies, cakes, and pies had been baked beforehand. Dozens of loaves of bread were ready; a bushel of potatoes had to be peeled. Long plank tables were set up on the lawn, and a washboiler full of steaming hot coffee was set out, with all the other food. The dinner was a jolly affair, much more like a social gathering than a work day. Laughter and gaiety were everywhere; even the dogs were infected, and ran around and around in circles yapping, enjoying each other's company. Children ran about munching on fried cakes, and wondering when their turn would come. And would there be anything left, the way those men were stuffing it in? Women bustled about, serving, and the men laughed and joked with them as they passed heaping dishes of food.

Brother Ole had bought kegs of beer, as was the custom, and the day got merrier and merrier. By night the main part of the barn was finished, and we were mighty proud that when the June hay crop was ready, we had a fine new red barn to put it in. Somehow, a big barn was evidence that you were over the hump, financially. This barn still stands and is in use, dwarfing the little log house, which even to this day serves as the dwelling house for the farmer who owns the place.

During the Christmas holidays, my folks always had a real party. Then everyone would drink the malt beer and homemade wine that Mother had made, and eat of all the good food she had been preparing for weeks. Then they would talk about Norway, and after a while it would get pretty lively. The men would, at least. If the downstairs of our little house got too crowded, the men would take off to the upstairs where they could smoke and drink and play cards in peace. They played mostly euchre and pedro, but I never heard that there was any gambling amongst our people.

Since nearly every family had from seven to twelve children, it was an unusual child who couldn't find a partner her own age. When Uncle Ole Böe and Aunt Aslaug came, I would take Anne, and my sister Sena would take Signe and Gurina. The boys would have John and Henry, and in their youth, Andres, who later died of smallpox. These friendships kept up all our lives, some for ninety-five years.

The malt beer that Mother served so freely was made of hops, malt, syrup or molasses, and water according to the other ingredients. They made the malt themselves, out of barley. It was first wet, then laid in a dry warm place until it started to sprout. After the malt was made, it was boiled with other ingredients, then strained and yeast added to make the brew "work" for a few days. She then skimmed off the yeast and put the brew in kegs. This crude beer was just a mild drink. You could take any amount of it and never even get lightheaded.

WELL, NO ONE ever came in to our house but he had to have a drink of this good beer, and no one liked it better than an old Irish neighbor, Matt Nesbitt, who lived up the road about a quarter of a mile to the west. After he had drunk his glassful, he would smack his lips and say, "Da Da." I suppose that meant "thanks" in Irish.

This Nesbitt family had come over from Ireland some time after our folks came from Norway, and their English was very broken. Our folks did not speak English at all, and you would think that they could never have had anything to do with each other. Besides, we were staunch Lutherans, and they were Irish Catholics. Two greater barriers than speech and religion could not be imagined.

But, it was not long before they were fast friends. I suppose it came from the mutual help they needed in those early days—sickness, trouble, harvesting, and just plain lonesomeness. Whenever Matt and his good wife, Maggie, came to visit, a child would have to stand by to interpret, and you can believe we had a time keeping our faces straight. But Mother's sharp eye was upon us, and it kept us sober through the ordeal. Whenever Matt came and sat down, folded his long legs one over the other, stroked his full black beard, and began his thick Irish immigrant speech, Mother would hurry down the steep cellar steps for several flagons of this homemade beer. Matt would click his tongue again and again and say, "Da Da," the while nodding his head in highest approval, his blue eyes snapping merrily. Then he would turn to Father and say, "By Judas, Mathis, an' if this isn't the best bee-ee-er-r-r I ever-r-r dr-r-rank." The unfortunate child interpreter would have to choke back her giggles and tell Father respectfully what the Irishman had said. As soon as she could, she would make her exit outdoors, where she could laugh for all she was worth.

These two barriers, language and religion, could not keep them from being the closest of friends for forty years. My folks had always a horror of the terrible "Katoliks." Yet here was a devout Catholic family, with their rosaries, crucifixes, and holy water, who were so utterly kind and loving that my people lost their fear of the Catholic religion, and a beautiful lesson in tolerance was learned on both sides.

Maggie was a well-built sturdy woman, with curling black hair and mild blue eyes that almost never smiled. But she was one of the kindest persons I ever knew. She raised her six children in a loving manner, and bore her immigrant poverty without complaint. Whenever we children went there, she had something for us, a tomato, an apple, or a cookie.

Every time there was a thunderstorm, old Maggie would sprinkle holy water over the whole house and everybody in it. If they were eating at our house on Friday, they would never touch meat, no matter how good it was, but Mother would remember to put on some pickled herring for them. To make it even nicer, Maggie was not dirty, as were some of the Irish immigrants, but was so clean that her unpainted floors shone white as sand from scrubbing. Mother soon came to realize that these Catholics worshipped the same God as she, and had just as good a chance of eternal salvation. She would nod her head firmly, in discussion with other stubborn Lutherans and say, *"Dersom nokken bliver salig, saa er det den gamle Nesbitt kjerringa."* (If anyone goes to Heaven, it will be that old Mrs. Nesbitt.)

Their son, Jim, was just like Maggie. He bought the old home place from his folks after he married, and took care of them tenderly while they lived. I will tell you about his wedding to the Irish Ella in a later chapter.

Across the road and up a ways from the Nesbitt's lived a Norwegian neighbor, Ole Stromme, whose farm adjoined ours. He was also from Telemarken, which gave us all a good start in friendship right away. He and his wife, Yli Haugen (pronounced Eelee; she changed it to Ellen because the Yankees called her Wiley), were the first couple to be married in the Winchester church, about fifteen years before our folks came. By the time Father and Mother got here, the Strommes already had many children and did not stop until they had thirteen in all.

Mr. Stromme came to our house so frequently that he was often there at mealtime. I think he must have managed it purposely sometimes, for he craved the old Norwegian cheeses that Mother made in such quantities. *Gammelost* was his favorite. He thought it was not fit to eat until it had turned yellow and green, and it was he that always said so vehemently,

> When the cheese is so old
> That it is green and gold,
> Then it is good.

And after every meal he ate at our house, he would say with emphasis, "This was the best meal I ever ate in my living time!" We children knew what was coming each time, and we would try to get out of the house before he came to his pet sayings.

There was quite a ceremony attached to eating even a simple meal among the Norwegians, and it all stemmed from the idea that food was a gift of God. Before the meal was begun, this prayer was usually said by Father (I'll translate it freely):

> In Jesus' name we go to the board
> To feast and drink upon His Word;
> God to be honored, us to be given,
> So have we food in the name of Heaven.

It was the mother's duty to press food upon her guest again and again, saying, "*Vaer saa god*" (Be so good). When a guest had had enough, he would lay his hand lightly on the stomach and say, "*Nei tak, jeg er mett*," which meant, "No, thanks, I have enough." When the meal was finished, the guest stood and went to the back of his chair, put his hands upon it, bowed to the hostess and said, "*Tak for maten*" (Thanks for the food). To omit any part of these ceremonies was to admit that you didn't come from nice people, and you can believe Ole Stromme never left any one of them off.

He was about the smartest man in the neighborhood, being at

various times justice of the peace, town clerk, and constable. His conversation was always sparkling with interest and news, light-hearted and interesting. This made a great contrast to my gentle, retiring, home-loving father, who would sit and chuckle and look forward to seeing that big tall slim man standing in the door with his cheerful *"God dag"* (Good day). Mother had more to say than Father as she bustled about the kitchen getting the meal. Since Ole Stromme was noted for his ability to embroider a tale, and she was a stickler for truth, Mother would argue with him, question him, and advise him. He would argue back good-naturedly. Father would sit and laugh, siding first with one than the other, saying, *"Ja ja ja. Visst er det saa"* (Yes, that surely must be so).

Mother would never quarrel with anyone, especially if he were a guest in her house, but if Stromme's tales got too fantastic, and she really couldn't believe what he was saying, she would shake her head and say, "Oh, yes, perhaps you are right," and bustle off to her cupboard corner where she would stir something vigorously in a bowl. Or perhaps she would hurry down the cellar steps after cheese or clotted cream. When she came back, she would have besides a pitcher of beer. This she would pour in two glasses for the men. The two old friends would take them in their hands, touch the rims together, smile at each other, and say, *"Skaal"* (Here's to you) before they drank.

Ellen Stromme did not come to our house very often, because she had this large family of children to take care of. But despite all her many activities, she occasionally found time in summer to walk down that dusty road with a milk-pail full of delicious yellow harvest apples. Whenever Ellen had a new baby, Mother would cook up a big two-quart pan of *römmegröt*, whose top floated with yellow butterfat, stick it full of sugar lumps, sprinkle it with cinnamon, wrap it in a clean cloth, and take it to her. Then they would have a good visit, and Mother would pronounce the new little one the prettiest of the lot. The women of our day had plenty of reason to stay home and tend to business, and did a good job of it. Ellen Stromme disciplined her thirteen children so strictly that they obeyed her without question. You really have to have control when you have so many, or they will run over you completely.

When Tone became a widow, she had to go to Stromme's often on business, because Ole Stromme always held some kind of town office like clerk, or treasurer. She may have gone there in regard to her pension, I don't know. Anyway, she used to tell us what a wonderful behaving family the Strommes were. In those days nearly all farmers had a sort of plain wooden bench with a flat-spindled back, sitting in the kitchen-living-dining room, which was used as a settee during the daytime. At night the cover was lifted up and there was a wooden pin to hold it. Then the front of the bench was pulled forward like a modern bed-lounge, until with it and the body of the bench, you had a box that would make a bed for two or more children. There was a straw or husk mattress in it that was undoubled, and quilts and pillows that made up the bed would be brought down from the chests upstairs. This bench was about six feet long, and Tone always told me how it would be ab-solutely filled with Stromme children. They would sit there every one of them so nice and clean and as quiet as a mouse the whole time she was there. Tone used to think that was a wonderful sight.

I will tell you here a story about Tone. She was a good one. One day she had bought a little pig from Stromme. She used to walk everywhere she went in those days, and a pig could not stop the healthy, strong-minded Tone. She put him in a gunny sack and carried him home three miles on her back.

Going back to Ole Stromme: One time he was working on the road some distance from home when he was suddenly stricken with terrible stomach cramps; he was so ill that he thought he was going to die. It might have been appendicitis, I don't know. He immedi-ately made this remark, "If I could only see Ellen before I go." She was the love of his life, and he protected her like a queen, with immense respect and honor, and she felt the same way about him.

The Stromme children were unusually bright. All the other girls around our town could do nothing but housework when they grew up, as none of them had any more education than what we called "common country school," and very few finished that. But Martha, one of the Stromme girls, even went to the State Normal School at Oshkosh. In those days, if you had a few weeks at the Normal School after you finished country school, and could stand an examination, you could get a diploma to teach in the country. As far as I remember the only studies in these schools were reading, writing, spelling, arithmetic, geography, and Constitution. Martha got her diploma and taught school. We were all so proud of her. Later she married a man who had a farm in Elbow Lake, Minnesota. When they got out there, she got the job of county superintendent.

Another of the children, Peer, was a wonder for those days. He first studied to be a minister, but after a few years in the work, he said, "I just cannot stand to be responsible for everybody's soul." So he quit preaching. He taught some, and then became the editor of a Norwegian paper called *Nordmanden* (The Norwegian). He had the wanderlust so badly that he crossed the ocean four times. Once he even went to China. There he got some pancakes that he simply could not eat. So he dropped them stealthily in his pocket, one by one, until he got out of his host's sight. Another time he was visiting up in the mountains of Norway, and thought he'd look in on a *seter*, to see what they were like, after hearing so much about them all his life. He knocked at the door, and expected to see a pretty rosy-cheeked girl, but instead there stood an old wrinkled woman. He never got over that disappointment, he said.

"A rolling stone gathers no moss," the old saying goes. This is what happened to Peer Stromme. He had had a very interesting life, but in his later years there were no savings. Besides that, he said in his book, he had two diseases that raced to see which was going to get him first. While he was living in Madison, Wisconsin, he began to write a book about his life (in Norwegian, of course), so that his dear wife, Laura, would have something to live on when he was gone. It proved to be the best thing he ever did, and it sold for five dollars a book. Many, many were sold in Winchester, you can believe. You could die laughing, reading that book, it is so funny. It is especially amusing to us old Norwegians because he tells about the people we knew so well, and of his own crazy doings. In vain did I search through it to see if he mentioned my folks, but he had not. In fact he didn't mention any of the neighbors but the midwife who officiated at his birth, and later knit mittens for him when he went to school. Being one of the oldest Stromme children, he was gone before my folks got to America, or soon after, since he left home at the age of twelve to go to school at Decorah, Iowa. I remember him, just faintly, coming home on visits.

The youngest brother of the Stromme family went to school in Madison, where Peer was living. He is now a district attorney out in Minnesota somewhere. Another brother is a banker.

Peer mentioned in his book something that we thought was very strange. His step-grandfather was a carpenter, and for that reason everyone called him "Peer Snekker" (Peer Carpenter). Peer says that on the gravestone in Winchester churchyard, this man's name stands just plain "Peer Snekker." That sounds odd for one who had a perfectly good family name. We still have in our family a large pine desk which Peer Snekker made for Tone and Hans.

I SUPPOSE OUR most remarkable neighbor was the one whose farm joined ours just over the high hill. This was the little hunchback, Peder Lund. The farm had formerly belonged to a Civil War widow named Bergit Hanson, who had four children. Besides the farm, she got a pension for herself and the children until they were a certain age. I guess she got along fairly well alone, but it must have been hard enough while the children were growing up.

So to our town came this small Norwegian man, who had been so crippled with some kind of rheumatism when he was eleven years old that he had a big hump on his back and chest. Both his head and arms were the same size as any other grown-up man, but his legs were so short that I don't believe he could have been over four feet tall. Because of this deformity, his parents in Norway had educated him very well. When he came to this country, he taught parochial school, and boarded with the Widow Hanson. Before anyone knew it, they were married. There were four children born to this union, and a better father, husband, and stepfather has never lived, I am sure. Not only was he good, but he was smart, and like Ole Stromme, held many town jobs, like assessor, clerk, and so on. After he married, he did not teach school any more, but managed the farm. Even though he could not do the work, he got other people to do it and managed it very well. He also taught night classes in the neighborhood.

Most important of all, he was made *klokker* (sexton) in our church, and held the position as long as he lived. This was an office next to the minister. At every occasion when an offering was taken for the minister—Easter, Pentecost, and Christmas—a smaller one was taken for the *klokker*. It was a very honored office. Peder rang the church bell, then marched down the aisle with his hymnbook under his arm, and sat in the front seat. He prayed the opening prayer in a loud ringing voice that all could hear. It was his duty, as well, to announce and lead the hymns, and one could hear his clear, melodious voice above all others. Despite his small stature, when most of our men were great, tall, husky people, no one ever treated Peder Lund lightly. He was highly respected, and we children were afraid of those beetling black brows that could take on a fierce look at times. When they looked as if they were going to meet in the middle over his long straight nose, everybody obeyed instantly. Just as like as not he would then find something funny to do or say that would make him chuckle and laugh until his whole body and beard and great shaggy head shook.

Peder was another frequent visitor at our house. He was fond of coming down the hill in the afternoon, about the time he knew Mother would be going out to the woodpile and picking up a pan of chips to build a quick sharp fire that would last just long enough to make a pot of coffee. Then out would come the bowl of lump sugar, a pitcher of rich, thick cream, and a plate of crispy cream cookies. The three of them, Father, Mother, and Peder, would sit around the table, suck their coffee-soaked sugar lumps and sip their coffee to their heart's content.

Peder would usually have some new story to tell out of a book he'd been reading; or they would tell each other tales of their happy young lives in Norway, their journey to this hard new country, and their troubles. He had more jokes than anyone of our neighbors, too. Peder came from Toten, in Norway, which was far away from Telemarken. So they had lots to tell each other that was interesting, and it never grew old or came to an end. It was when Bergit Lund came along, that Mother and she would go into a corner and smoke their clay pipes and cry for the Old Country. Bergit and she were from the same place over there.

In sickness, there was no one like Peder Lund. There was never anyone sick in the neighborhood for miles around that he would not appear at the door. He sat by the bedside and ministered comfort faithfully and regularly, praying and singing with his beautiful voice, until the sick one either got well or died. When Lena and Kristine had diphtheria, none of our relatives dared to come near, because they all had small children. Peder had little ones, too, but he came to our house regularly. He would sit by Kristine's bed and sing to her and comfort her.

When she died, he took up her hand and said, *"Du yndig blomst, som her er bukket"* (You lovely flower, that has wilted here.) Only Peder could think of those sweet beautiful words to say on every occasion.

At another time, when Anne and Halvor Johnson had just lost two children of typhoid fever, and Anne herself was in bed with the same sickness, he sat by her bed and sang this beautiful hymn:

> *Her er kaldt og ude stormen truer,*
> *Men i Himmelen der er alt saa smukt.*
> *O, jeg er saa træt, maa öiet lukke;*
> *Moder, se nu kysser englen mig.*

> (Here it is cold, and outside the storm is raging,
> But in Heaven everything is so full of beauty.
> Oh, I am so tired, my eyes are closing;
> Mother, see the angel is kissing me.)

WHAT MATT NESBITT and Ole Stromme and Peder Lund must have meant to my folks, no one will ever know, and since they came to see us so often, our folks must have meant a lot to them. I was always proud and fond of my parents. Some of the younger set around our town that did not think much of church or religion used to call Mother "the Holy One." She would read her Bible as long as her eyesight allowed her, and that was after she was ninety years old. She had to use eyeglasses quite a few years before that, some she got after "Anne-to-Torger," when she died. They were very small steel-bowed spectacles, and Mother could see with them just fine.

Father was the same staunch Christian. He went to church as long as he was able to walk up the steps to it. In his last year (at ninety-three) he was losing his sight, and my daughter, Erna, who was just a little girl, was left with them during vacation so that she could lead him around the farm, for he still had to see how things were going. Every day after dinner, he would have to take a nap, as he had all his life, and it was her job to lead him to the place beside the barn where the straw-stacks were. Where the sun had been in the morning, it would still be dry and warm, but the shadow of the stack would now protect him as he slept. Mother would always motion Erna back as they started out on this trip, and whisper, "Watch his mouth. He sleeps with it open. Do not let an *orm* crawl in." Erna never took her eyes off that round mouth, sucking in and out over toothless gums, all during those naps.

I shall never forget his sweet voice in the mornings. Mother sang now and then, as she went about her work, too. One of her favorite hymns went like this:

> Oh, you who go in the links of sin
> If you knew how hard it is in Satan's slavery
> You would then instantly stop and think
> And seek the One who could make you free.
> What joy God's angels would receive
> If you would begin immediately.

I never heard my parents quarrel. She was sharp-tongued sometimes, but he never answered back. To hear them talking and visiting together, you would have thought them two old friends instead of man and wife. They seemed to consider it a joy to help each other. After Father's health failed somewhat, he would not lie in the bedroom, but wanted to stay with her in the kitchen all day, where he had a couch to rest on. His hearing was as keen as ever, so they could visit back and forth while she did her work. When she passed him, he would often murmur, "Thorild, my Thorild." She would reply, "Mathis." Until he could no longer stumble up the steps, he carried in wood and water for her and saw that there was plenty of kindling to build fires with in the morning. It was surprising how many old couples in those times were really sweethearts to the very last days of their lives.

Peder Lund and Father lived close neighbors for forty-two years, and I can never remember a cross word between them. Father was in his last illness about two months, and Peder came every day, even though it was in bitter winter weather, and prayed and sang for him. This meant everything to Mother, because her heart was breaking to see her beloved Mathis dying. Not many of us children could stay there steadily because of our families.

When Father died, Peder was sitting by his bed, as usual. He got up after a while and went home, and said to his wife, "My old neighbor is gone, and I feel I shall soon follow him." She told us later that then he got his hymnbook and sang a hymn so loudly, that she had never heard him sing any louder.

Matt Nesbitt's son, Jim, who was then about forty years old, came to lay Father out, since nobody had undertakers in our part of the country. Tears streamed down his ruddy Irish face as he cared for the shrunken form he had known lovingly since childhood. He washed the body, shaved the face, and put a clean nightshirt on him. They had taken the bed out of the bedroom when Father died, and put a bench in there instead. Now Jim had him laid on this bench, put camphor-soaked cloths over Father's face to keep it from getting black, and laid a sheet over him. As he was about to leave, he took hold of the cold shrunken hand and said, "Faith an' this old hand niver-r-r hur-r-r-rt nothin' in all it's hull life."

Ole Stromme and Matt Nesbitt had died many years before, but Peder Lund came down the next day and insisted on going to Neenah, twelve miles away, with brother Ole to buy the coffin. Everybody protested at this, for it was the twenty-ninth of January and very cold. That was a bad winter, with so much snow and wind. Driving twenty-four miles over and back with horses and sleigh in those drifted roads would take a long time, several hours each way, they argued. But no matter how they pleaded with him, he was bound to go.

After the funeral, Peder took pleurisy and had a stroke of paralysis, and six weeks later he followed his old neighbor to the little graveyard beside the Winchester church.

113

Mother shook her sorrowing grey head from side to side when she heard the news of Peder's death. *"Ja, Mathis gav nok sin vandringstav til Peder"* (Yes, Mathis gave his pilgrim's staff to Peder).

So they lived and so they died, these four friends. The light-hearted Ole Stromme, loving Matt Nesbitt, learned Peder Lund, and quiet, gentle Mathis Kjeldalen. I know that in some quiet corner of Heaven, their friendship still goes on.

TONE

I HAVE MENTIONED several times that the families of my mother, Thorild, and my husband's mother, Tone, were greatly attracted to each other. The two sides were not in the least related, but lived near each other in the Old Country. Now Winchester Township in Wisconsin was full of them and their descendents. Some of the couples you have already heard about—Anne and Torger Landsverk, Uncle Ole Böe and Tone's sister Aslaug, Tone's brother Halvor and Mother's niece Anne. There were many other intermarriages. I do not know any two families that have had more except the kings and queens of Europe, and yet there was never a mentally defective child born, and only one crippled baby that I know of. They were almost all economically independent and kept out of jail, and there have been only three or four divorces that I remember in our whole relationship.

You can see how pretty nearly all who went to the Winchester church were related to each other, either by blood or by marriage. I could never understand how Mother could feel so homesick for Norway when she was surrounded by her own folks and acquaintances. That is, not until I got old myself and had to leave the home that I loved. Mother was thirty-eight when she came over, and that is quite old to transplant your whole life. I was seventy-four before I had to be uprooted, and I'll never forget my old home.

I want to explain here about Norwegian surnames. They are very confusing to people who have not been brought up with them. For Norwegians, a woman like my mother had had a terribly long list of names, but they trace her from the cradle to the grave. We all understood it, but the Yankees would throw up their hands in despair of ever unraveling it. Thorild was her Christian name. Her father's name was Andres, so she was Thorild Andresdatter. At successive times in her life, she bore the surnames of Böe, Leine, Juve, Kjeldalen, and Olson. Her father owned the Böe farm, therefore Böe placed her on the land. Then she married Mathis Olson (son of Ole), who lived on the Haevre farm. This made him Mathis Olson Haevre before his marriage. After he married, he bought the Leine farm, so he had to change his name and that of his family to Leine, and the Haevre was dropped. After a while he bought the Juve farm and lived on it until he came to America. Then Leine was forgotten. On all his sea chests and boxes was written in fine large painted script, "Mathis Olson Juve." He bought the Kjeldalen farm in Winchester, at which time he dropped the Juve name and was known thereafter as Kjeldalen—Mathis Olson Kjeldalen (always pronounced Cheldarn). Of course, his children were known as that, too. I was always Thurina Mathisdatter Kjeldalen among the Norwegians, and Tilla Olson to the Yankees.

These names were so confusing to the Yankees that most Norwegians changed them after a while. The distinctive names of Juve and Skare and Daalaan and Böe were dropped, and people went by their fathers' Christian names, such as Olson, Johnson, and Larsen. There are so many of these names now, that you can hardly keep the families straight. I have to stop and study it out every time I am introduced to a new young person. I believe it would have been better if they had kept their old names, with maybe changing the spelling.

I think I have told you about the given names being changed. Yankees tittered at Signe, Aslaug, and Bergit. So the poor girls in self-defence would begin calling themselves Sena, Alice, and Betsey instead. Now the old names are coming back, and we hear of Karens and Kristins with the good Old Country ring.

WHEN TONE came to America she was a plump young girl of nineteen, with flashing blue eyes, fine white skin, rosy cheeks, and a nose that was high and thin. She had an abundance of curling brown hair. Although she was never very tall, she was as strong as a heifer and snorted at weaklings who got tired, or had to take naps in the daytime. She always loved a good joke, and could laugh until she shook when amused. But she had one weakness, and that you will be surprised at. She cried for everything that happened and told her hard luck stories over and over all her life, being even worse than my mother this way.

Her first days in America were hard, without a doubt. Although her brothers Halvor and John and her sister Aslaug were as good to her as they could be, she did have to support herself. That meant she had to go out and do housework, as all immigrant girls did. Not knowing one word of English, she was put in a Yankee household.

One day the lady sent her down cellar after something, and Tone had not the slightest idea what it was. So she just stayed down there and cried. Pretty soon, down came the lady and asked her what was the matter. With much crying and pointing, Tone told her, and the trouble was righted, but Tone never forgot the experience.

Another time she happened to be out by the road when a Norwegian man went by. Somehow she got acquainted with him and watched for him every day when he passed, when she would run out and talk to him and cry and cry about her hard luck. It had been hard to leave her folks in Norway, especially that old, white-haired father. But she did have these other fond relatives here, and she was young and strong, with all her life before her. Besides, she was making more money than she ever had made in her life, and Tone loved money.

After a few years in America, Tone married Hans (Henry) Olsen Skare (pronounced Skah-ree), son of Torger's brother, Halvor. The spelling, "Oleson," came later through the decision of Captain Ole Oleson. In Norway, Hans would have been called Hans Halvorson Skare. But the immigrants dropped the custom of naming after their fathers' Christian names and the farm names as soon as they came to America. Since Halvor Olsson Skare was called both Halvor Olsson and Halvor Skare, his children took on his names, with varied spellings. Hans's name is given as "Henry Olsen" on his tombstone.

Hans was eighteen and Tone was twenty-one when they married. You must remember that children became grown-up a lot earlier than they do now. Hans, in particular, was very large— over six feet tall, and very good-looking. Tone was crazy about him. Very serious at times, Hans was full of tricks and liked his drink, as nearly everybody did. Drinks were cheap in those days, so I suppose that was one reason they used liquor so freely. Nearly everyone was poor to start with, but they always drank.

This Hans Olsen and my Uncle Ole Böe, who were neighbors and had married sisters, used to go on lots of sprees together. There was a great difference in their ages, but Hans was old for his age, and Uncle Ole was young for his. One particular time, I was told, these two men were on their way to Butte des Morts, a few miles away, where there were a couple of saloons. While they were driving along, there came a rich lady from Winneconne with a fast horse behind them. She was one who was noted far and wide for her haughty pride in passing people, but she did not get by Hans. He was driving his own fast nag. Every time she got up to these men and wanted to pass, Hans whipped up and took a sprint ahead, and so it went all the way to the village. When they got there, she came galloping up, jumped out with the horsewhip in her hand and was going to flay Hans. This infuriated him so that he was going to charge her and take the whip away. It took two men, one of them "Ole Ox" to hold him until she could drive safely off. Hans did not realize when he named Uncle "Ole Ox" that that great strength would be used on him one day.

Hans was a very hard-working man, however, and was a favorite of his parents, Margit and Halvor. He worked the home farm on shares. Each family had its own living quarters in the log house. The old folks had the main part, kitchen, bedroom, and pantry, with the upstairs over that, as they had other children at that time. Hans and Tone had only one big room to live, eat, cook, and sleep in, with their three children. Two of the little ones slept in a trundle bed which was shoved under the big bed in the daytime. They got along very well, though, because both Hans and Tone were saving and hard-working. They bought forty extra acres of their own near by. Hans had a good business head, for all his youth. She was just as good in her housekeeping, saving and clever. She often told me that whatever he bought was of the best, poor as they were, and when he had a debt, he would "pick a penny here and a penny there" until he got hold of enough to pay it. Their children were named Mary, John, and Julia. It was Hans's wish that they have these English names so that they would not have to change them later, as other Norwegians did. He had to call himself "Henry" half the time.

It went well with Hans and Tone until the Civil War broke out. Then he had to go, and she was left alone with her three little ones. Mary was six, John about four, and Julia not quite two, all born in the log house. She lived in the same room she had when they were together, hoping and praying that he would soon come back to them. Tone was always a devout Christian, and now was when she had to put her trust in the Lord.

Hardly a Norwegian home but had someone in the Northern army. When Lincoln issued his second call for 500,000 volunteers, at least forty men went from the Winchester church. None of them had ever seen a Negro, probably, yet they went "to free the slaves." That was all they knew it was about. Being such great lovers of freedom as Scandinavians are, they could be appealed to easily on that score. I often wonder how they understood their English captain's commands, these immigrants.

Tone's brothers, Halvor and John, went. John had learned to be a drummer in the Norwegian army, so that was what he did here, and they said he was a dandy at it. Hans's brother Ole was on a gunboat on the Mississippi. Another soldier was the Kjeldalen who owned the farm Father bought when the man came back from war. The women were left to till the soil alone, with the help of old men and children, and their hearts bled with anxiety. Every now and then news would come that someone had died in Andersonville Prison, someone was killed in Sherman's campaign in Atlanta, someone was sick in a hospital in Ohio.

Hans was gone about two years and his family did not see him in all that time. Tone did not hear from him very often, either, and finally not at all. She was distracted, worrying where he was, and what was happening to him.

Then one day she happened to look up and saw him come walking, as thin as a skeleton. Wild with joy, she ran to open the gate for him, and found that he had walked the whole nine miles from Butte des Morts. Deathly sick he was by the time he got to the house and told them his story: While he was passing through a town in Alabama, he had gone into a restaurant and ordered a piece of pie. The proprietor must have put poison in it, for right after that he got a terrible bowel trouble, and barely made the trip home. He lived only three weeks after he got there, and Tone was nearly crazy with grief over her fine husband. When he died, some neighbors made a coffin for him, and he was buried in the graveyard by the Winchester church. You can see his grave to this day, with a small American flag waving over it. Tone grieved over him until her death, at the age of ninety-three, even though she married again after some years. Her second husband had to hear all about the wonderful Hans all his life, and see her point out the picture in his soldier uniform in the family album, while tears dropped at every mention of his name. She used to tell my children, when they asked her what Hans was like, "You remember Uncle Martin [his brother]? You know how handsome and tall and straight he was? Well, Hans was taller, and finer looking and better in every way than Martin."

Before he died, Hans had provided that she should keep on living in that same room on his father's farm until the children were old enough to help her. She had $8.00 a month pension for each of them until they should be sixteen or eighteen, and $12.00 for herself. She had three cows and some chickens and sheep that Hans had bought before he went to war, and she raised enough feed for them on her own forty acres. You can know that a girl who has grit enough to leave her parents and come to a strange land at the age of nineteen, would have enough to carry on by herself if she had to. It was while she was still a widow that she went to Ole Stromme's and carried the pig home on her back in a gunny sack, walking three miles. With the children's pension money and her own, she soon bought another forty acres adjoining the one she had, and even saved money besides. It did not take much to live in those days. She got so used to skimping in those hard years, that although she became quite well-to-do in later times, she never got over her thrifty habits. She applied them to a point of stinginess at the table, and my children would complain that she fed them spareribs on Easter, and salt pork at Christmas, if they were so unfortunate as to be there on those important days, when we at home were feasting on all the good things I always had on these occasions.

After seven years of widowhood, Tone married a quiet decent man named Joseph Olson, who was eleven years younger than she. Do you see what I mean by the mix-up with names in America? This Joseph was really an "Omness," and Hans was a "Skare," yet for the sake of the Americans, they both went by the name of Olson, and were not one bit related.

It used to be a mystery to us that Tone always married younger men. But she was little and cute and never showed her age. Joseph was an excellent carpenter. He built a log house for them on the second forty acres that she had bought with her pension money, and put up a cow stable, a horse stable, and a granary of logs.

Joseph was as different from Hans as night from day. Short of stature, with arms that came almost to his knees, he was slow-moving and speaking, as opposed to the tall, spirited, mischievous Hans. You could no more picture Joseph going off on a drinking spree than flapping his arms and flying. He was one of those who looked as if he had been born an old man. Tone was so quick that she could work circles around him. But he was very good to her and the children and was a steady worker, so they were quite happy all their lives. He had no money, but he was kind and helpful and very easy-going, and life was much easier for her than it had been all those years of war and widowhood.

As the children grew older, they got to where they could earn money for their own clothes. John was always a money-maker. Until he married, he gave all he earned to his mother, he loved her so much. He often told me that he did a man's work when he was thirteen years old. He did not get much schooling, and this was why: When he was only five years old, he was visiting his grandmother, Margit. While he was there, a terrible storm came up. Lightning struck the chimney of the house and tore it down, and part of the house was set on fire. At this, John got such a fear of lightning that whenever there was even a slight hint of a storm while he was in school, he would take his cap and race for home to take care of his mother. In this way, he kept falling behind in his class, and since he never did take to book-learning very well, he soon quit altogether. His mother needed him, anyway, to take the place of a man around the farm before she married. Lightning and Hell were the only two things John ever was afraid of. All our lives, when it began to blow and lightning he would get everybody up at night and make us sit up until it was all over.

After John was about nineteen he used to go every spring on what they called the "log drive." The northern part of Wisconsin was noted for its fine timber. Men from all over the country would come to work in the "pineries," cutting logs all winter, and hauling them to the nearest river on sleighs. In the early spring they would float them down the river to a place called Bay Boom.

They needed lots of strong young men to walk along the logs in the river, and keep them from getting into a jam. If this happened, the logs would pile up and refuse to move down the river. At Bay Boom John would have a few days' rest and go to see his mother, giving her all the money he had earned, even though she now had a husband to care for her. He had nothing saved up when we were married. He would work on this drive about two months every spring, and he said he never had dry clothes on him in all that time. They used to sleep along the river as they moved on, in tents, with only pine boughs for beds. In the morning in early spring, their clothes were frozen solid to their bodies. How they ever lived is beyond all understanding. But John was always as strong as a horse, and the only real sick spell he ever had in his life was his last illness of five weeks, when he was seventy-nine.

While he was on the log drives, he made friends of the Indians who were hired by the logging companies to follow the log drive in canoes. It was their job to fish the men out if they fell off the slippery logs. Many of the men treated the Indians mean, and believe me, they could flounder around and almost drown before the Indians picked them up. But John, who had such a friendly, jolly way, had learned a little of their lingo. He would say, "Bezhoo" (*bon jour*, good day) and "M'see (*merci*, thanks). John would hardly hit the water before the Indians would be there lifting him out.

John had a rich uncle, Ole Oleson (the brother of Hans), who lived in Oshkosh. It was this same Ole who had fought on a gunboat during the Civil War and was said to have been at the fall of New Orleans. I suppose this is where he got his interest in boats, for when he returned, he became a boat captain and went by the name of Captain Ole Oleson. He was married to the only daughter of an aristocratic innkeeper by the name of Petford in Butte des Morts. This Mary Ann was a great beauty, and she and Ole had an only daughter named Erna, who was noted for her prettiness, as well she might be with such handsome parents. She sponsored the battleship "Wisconsin" when it was launched.

Now Uncle Ole Oleson thought a great deal of my John and tried to take a father's place with him. Every spring he wanted him as soon as he got off the log drive. Captain Oleson then had a tug-boat of his own, and he made John the engineer. They towed logs from Bay Boom to the Oshkosh and Fond du Lac sawmills until the lake froze over in the fall. Their route led past the place where our daughter Erna now has a summer cabin on Lake Winnebago, near Oshkosh. John used to stand on the shore when he visited her, point out the way they used to tow the logs, then turn sadly to her and say, "How on earth could you buy a place on this ter-ribly stormy lake? Why didn't you buy up at Waupaca, where its *real* camping ground!" How he loved that Waupaca!

John gave all the money he earned during the summers to his mother, too; it was a big help for her to put it in the farm and more buildings. John was always on hand to help build. They had so many buildings on the place at last that one of their friends called it Butte des Morts, because it looked like a little village. In the winter John stayed home and helped his folks with chores, hauled hay from the marsh where it had been put in stacks in the sum-mer, and wood out of a swamp about eight miles from home. Most all of the farmers around there had bought from six to ten acres of this swamp. It was covered with tamarack and other trees. They would cut enough for a load and make only one trip a day, haul-ing wood home to last them through the whole year. During the winter, John helped his stepfather make sleighs and hayracks and other things they might need. He sold some sleighs, or rather ex-changed them for a new cutter and a new single harness for his folks. Whenever there was a big job, like ditching or building, he was the one that had to figure it out and do most of the work. There never was a son that sacrificed so willingly for his folks as my John.

TONE HAD ONE sister, Ingeborg, who had a boy that I want to men-tion. He was one of twelve children. When Björn (which means "bear") was just a young boy he came over from Norway with his parents, three brothers, and a sister. Soon he changed his name to Barney, but kept his surname of Barstad. He was an exceptionally bright boy, and a character you don't often find. When he was only a youngster, he began to drink and dance, and even have a sweetheart. After a while he and some other young men from the vicinity took a notion to go out West. His mother was in bed with her last illness at the time, and he did not have the courage to tell her that he was leaving. Therefore, he just sneaked away. Barney was her baby, and they never saw each other again, as she died a few months later.

Out West these young men got jobs on a railroad, working on a section. Barney got in with a tough bunch, and he drank worse than ever. The rumors went that they even had planned to hold up the train but got so drunk that they went to sleep and the train whizzed past them.

It happened that one of the gang left the others at a certain time each night and went into the woods near by. Barney got curious about it and followed him. He found him kneeling in prayer and talked to him. The boy asked Barney if he would not pray, too, but the reply was, "Me, pray? God would not listen to a sinner like me."

"Yes," the fellow said, "that is the kind God listens to."

Barney went away shaking his head. God would never listen to anyone who would leave his mother on her deathbed and do all the things he did.

A little later this fellow got Barney to go into a religious meeting in town, a sort of revival meeting. The minister was saying how Jesus wanted sinners to come to him. Barney still could not believe it, but he kept going, and one night he heard the words that convinced him. He began to pray for himself, and to believe in Christ. He made up his mind that he would spend the rest of his life serving the Lord, and he lost no time in carrying it out. Soon he was in Red Wing Seminary, studying to be a minister. He went through with his studies and became a very good preacher, serving several congregations well.

About the time he was converted, he happened to go to another revival meeting, Salvation Army, I think. And there was a girl singing in the sweetest voice he had ever heard. Never one to hang back, Barney got acquainted with her, and it was not very long before they were married. They were very happy, and had four nice children.

I remember what a to-do there was in the old Lutheran church in Winchester when Barney came back to preach. He had gone away a wild young boy and was now a highly respected, full-fledged minister of the Lutheran church. He told the tale of how he left his mother on her deathbed and of his conversion. It was very touching. Another time when he came back, they got all the relatives together and took a panorama picture on the lawn of Uncle Ole Böe's daughter Anne, who had married Henry Larsen. Tone was sitting right in the middle of it, right by him in his mother's place. She looks just like Queen Victoria, and she was as proud as a queen of her nephew that had become a minister.

One time Barney came to visit John and me when we lived near Oshkosh. He was a short, stout man with a full beard, and he was lots of fun. He visited with us all evening, said prayers for us, and then left, asking us to take God with us wherever we went. I guess the poor man had learned what it was to go without God.

Those Barstads were a smart family. Barney had a brother Halvor who was the father of another Barney Barstad, still living, a successful lawyer in Superior, Wisconsin. He is lieutenant governor of the Northern Wisconsin-Michigan Division of the Kiwanis clubs. This man now spells his last name "Barstow."

TONE OWED MUCH of what she knew in life to her mother-in-law, Margit Skare, with whom she spent her first married life and widowhood. This Margit was an exceptional person. She was born in Norway, too, but had to go out working when very young. Margit was short in stature, not at all pretty, but she was sturdy and strong, and she could do anything that was laid before her hands. Even as a girl, she had a way of wearing her simple clothes so that they looked fashionable on her, and she had such a way of managing people that she made friends wherever she went.

Her first job was with the Skare family, who were fairly well to do. Torger Landsverk was one of the boys. I suppose he got the name Landsverk from a farm he owned after he married. He had a brother named Halvor, who fell in love with Margit. Now, as this girl came from a poor family, and people were supposed to marry in their own class over there, old Father Skare rather disapproved of the love affair. Even he, though, could not help liking her. Because of the stylish way she dressed and wore her hair, he gave her a Norwegian nickname, "Stasbot" (Style Patch), which they often named a dainty spotted cow. Quick as a wink she came right back at him with "Burman," which was a favorite name for a fine bull, as "Ferdinand" is in our day. One day Father Skare started to tease her, and she playfully offered to wrestle with him. "Shall Burman and Stasbot lock horns?" she said. This was a trifle bold, but she got away with it. It was good enough for him, and so he left her alone.

Margit married Halvor a little later, but it was a sad match. He wasn't half as good as she, for all his money. They came to America after a few years. On the way over a certain woman had a baby and died on ship-board. Margit took the baby and raised it as her own. She made no difference between little Sena and her own flock. Margit and Halvor settled on a farm about two miles from the Winchester church.

I am almost ashamed to tell you that this Halvor was known as "the meanest man on earth." He was so jealous, lazy, cruel, and drunken, that he brought Margit nothing but misery. It would have killed an ordinary woman, but Margit took it, and stood it. Not only did she triumph over this miserable marriage, but she was one whose spirit could overcome a homely face. Her mouth and nose were large, and the eyes were a sort of common grey. But after people had been with her a few minutes, somehow that homely face became beautiful. Her personality shone right through it. The long struggle with Halvor never soured her. It seemed rather to bring out every bit of fineness in her, developed all her clever traits, and made her a diplomat of the first order.

As mean as he was, Halvor did not completely conquer her. One day Joseph was working there, and Halvor sat down to the table, whining as usual. "Oh, if I could only eat as you eat, it would be fun!" he said to Joseph.

This made Margit hopping mad. She stood up and pointed to the door. "You scoundrel," she cried. "Here you came in an hour ago and demanded a big bowl of cream and bread and sugar and stuffed yourself. Now you whine to the people that you are not able to eat. Get out of that door, and stay out." And he did.

Halvor was always in a fight of some sort. One time he had got in trouble with Uncle Ole Böe, and came panting home saying that he was after him to lick him. This was really serious, because Halvor was as tall and thin as a pole, and Ole Böe was "Ole Ox." With fear and trembling, Halvor hid himself in the bedroom. After a while Uncle Ole came walking into the yard, fiery mad. When Margit saw him coming, she took the water pail and went out to the pump, and was pumping peacefully when he came up. She let on that nothing was the matter, and in her kind, gentle, winning way, began to talk of something else. She had such a wonderful way of expressing herself, that before they got into the house, she had him all out of the notion of a fight. They had a lovely time talking, and eating doughnuts and coffee, while Halvor sweated and trembled in the closet.

Halvor and Margit had four boys and two girls, besides the little Sena they raised. The boys were Captain Ole Oleson, Captain Martin Oleson, John, Hans (my husband's father), and the girls, Anna and Emmeline. These children almost worshipped their mother. When I came into the family, Margit had become rather fat, but was still stylish, and excelled in needlework and dressmaking. She would smile at me in her ladylike way and say, "It is pleasant to see someone who keeps herself as nice as you after she is married." She knew just how to take everyone so that they loved her, and could get along with everybody on earth except her husband. She used to pray for a little peace from him before she died. The Lord must have loved her, too, for she outlived Halvor seventeen years, the fine sons showering her with every luxury they could lay their hands on.

It was her wonderful management of the family that saved them from being mean like their father. Until the boys were grown, she made them mind as when they were little, but they did not resent being bossed by this little mother of theirs. Captain Ole was her most famous son. Martin was a boat captain, also, and became a well-to-do man. Her son, John, worked on a tugboat, too, but one morning he was found dead on it. Nobody knew if he was struck by lightning, or had a heart attack. I have told you how Hans died during the Civil War.

The daughter, Anna, was a very comely woman, and had inherited her mother's capable ways. But at the age of fifteen she made the great mistake of marrying the wrong man. I can't understand how Margit allowed this, but probably it wasn't too pleasant for the girl around home with Halvor. It wouldn't have been too bad if the man had been worth anything. But he drank and was so lazy that Anna and their three children almost starved to death. Often she had to go out to work to support them. People said that she could be trusted for a bag of flour at the store, but that he couldn't.

I do not know how it was that this Oleson family was always mixed up with boats. One time this husband of Anna's got a job as engineer on a tugboat. It was his duty to see to it that there was plenty of water in the boiler at all times, for there must be steam to run the boat. One day there was a terrible explosion, and everything was blown to pieces. He was thrown into the water. People said that the minute they pulled him out, he held up two fingers as a measure and gasped, "Just before she blew up—I looked at the gauge—and there was THIS much pressure!" Nobody believed him. They said he could not have tended the boiler properly. That was the end of his engineering.

Anna stood this kind of treatment for several years then left him, taking the children with her. He went out to Minnesota and bought a farm, and after a while persuaded her to come out to live with him. She went, hoping that he had reformed, but it was the same thing again. So one day, while he was in town, she took her children and left for good. He remarked then, "I once had a good-looking woman, but could not keep her. Now I will marry the homeliest woman I can find. Maybe she will stay with me." I never heard if he found that woman or not.

Anna never married again, although she had many chances. She raised the children herself, and one of them became a very high official of the Elgin Watch Company. The last we heard of Anna she was in California. She had turned spiritualist and was peddling pamphlets from door to door which proclaimed the end of the world. She died out West somewhere.

Emmeline was the baby of Margit's family. She married a good man and was happy all her life with him. Here again the family was mixed up with boats. Harry, one of her sons, was crazy about them, so a son of his Uncle Martin's allowed him to work on his boat. Harry was supposed to tend couplings, but there was a huge rope, a tow line, that wound around a big wheel when they did a certain kind of work. Harry could never leave this rope alone, no matter how much they warned him. He would cup his hands around it, and was fascinated to see it slide through them. One day they heard a terrible squeal, like a bunch of cats, and when they came running, they found that Harry had been wound up around the wheel with the rope. They got him out some way and he was taken home. The doctor said there was nothing to be done for him, and he died in a few hours.

But it was Captain Ole Oleson of whom Margit was the most proud. It was he who was the first to change the spelling of their name from Olson to Oleson, which he argued was the true spelling, since it meant "Son of Ole." He had very little education, maybe a few terms in country school, but was naturally bright, like his mother. The Skares were very smart people, too. When the Civil War broke out, Ole joined the U.S. Navy, and was on a gunboat that went up and down the Mississippi River. It was said that he was at the siege of New Orleans. When he came back he got a job on a tugboat in Oshkosh. In the winter, when the water froze over, he went to business college, and learned to write, spell, and figure very well. He was an especially fine writer, something very important in the days before typewriters. He got to be captain of that boat, later bought it, and was always known after that as Captain Ole Oleson. He was a fine figure of a man, over six feet tall, with strong even features, thick brown hair, slightly balding, and a heavy shining brown moustache. He had a most engaging personality, like his mother. But the most important thing about his looks was those keen blue eyes, looking out at you from under bristling brown brows. The Skare brows always grew down, instead of sideways. Oh, those foxy Skare eyes that the women were so crazy over! You can see them in my great-grandsons.

When Hans died, Ole tried to take his place with my John, and when he was old enough, had him come to be engineer on his boat for several summers. Ole got in with some very rich lumbermen while he pulled their logs from Bay Boom to their sawmills in Oshkosh with his tugboat, and he made a lot of money himself. One of these men was old Mr. Philetus Sawyer, who had made millions buying up the virgin timberland in northern Wisconsin. He and Ole became bosom friends, and had lovely homes not far apart on Algoma Street in Oshkosh. In a few years he helped Ole to get the office of postmaster in Oshkosh. In those early days it was a very exalted position "by appointment of Presidents Harrison and McKinley," and Ole held it with distinction for eight years. In a book we still have, called *Oshkosh of Today* (1898), his picture and write-up take up more space than anyone's except the President of the Normal School and one famous woman teacher.

It was while working up and down the river on the boat, that John used to eat a certain kind of hash that he never forgot, and always wanted me to make after we were married. I tried and tried, but although he liked my hash very well, he would always say it wasn't quite like what they used to eat on the boat.

One night I put three or four cut onions on in a little water to boil in the frying pan. Then I added a lot of chopped roast beef. While that was simmering together, I chopped boiled potatoes fine, added them, seasoned them with salt and pepper and let them cook together for a little while. It was almost like I had always made hash, but I guess it was sort of mushy-like, more than usual. After John had eaten the first forkful, he turned to me with eyes lit up, and a look of utter delight on his face. "Ma!" he cried, "It's Tugboat Hash!" My children never will forget that moment, after hearing about that hash all their lives.

It was during these boat days, too, that John saw in some captain's cabin, a long carved wooden chain with an anchor on one end and a pilot wheel on the other. It so struck his fancy that he never gave up mentioning it through the years. When he was seventy years old, and had retired from all his activities, he got himself some soft pine and began to whittle. He did not stop until he had made a wonderful carved chain, anchor, and wheel for himself (seventeen feet long) and a six-foot chain, anchor, and wheel, for every one of his children. It was the joy and pride of his life to visit them and see those chains hung over their mantles or chests in their homes.

I WILL TELL you about Tone's last days. She was really a cute little woman all her life. She had the most beautiful complexion of anyone around—it was pink and white until her death. She told me once that she had never put soap on it in all her life. Her years of working out in Yankee households made her much more up to date than my mother, and I think my children enjoyed her more. Margit, her stylish mother-in-law, taught her how to dress so that she was always picturesque, even in her everyday clothes. In the later days, when other old ladies disfigured themselves with bobbed hair and showed their knobby old legs in short skirts, Tone kept to her full floor-length skirts and her tight little waists with high collars and long sleeves. As her hair whitened, she took to black caps with lace on them, and her bonnets were the same black plumed affairs she had worn in her early married life. She kept up the hard-luck stories all her life, however, and would tell them to any stranger: how she was left with "three little bits of ones when her man died." Whereas my mother had it easy until she was thirty-eight, and had to struggle after that, Tone's life was all hardship until that age, and from then on she was well off. But she never left off crying and telling the old stories. When she wasn't crying, however, she was full of life and laughter and pep, and when she and Joseph retired to Winneconne, she was "Grandma" to the whole village. She was what you could call a picture-book grandma.

Her English always remained something amusing. She could express herself very well, with the aid of a few Norwegian words here and there and a burst of laughter in a tight spot. To the end of her days she said, "iffy I," for "if I," and "rat's it," for "that's it."

Her house was always neat and fairly clean up to her death. She had a way of fixing it, learned in the Yankee households, that created a picture when you came in. First she would take you into the guest bedroom beside the entrance where there was a varnished pine bedroom set. It was decorated in blue medallions, centered with a lovely hand-painted head of a Colonial lady. Off this was a large closet with a window, where she kept the pine desk that Peer Snekker had made for her and Hans. In the top of this she kept papers and old buttons and all kinds of junk. Every drawer was full, because she couldn't throw anything away. In one of the three big drawers in the bottom she kept the clothes she was to be laid out in. When she came to spend the winter with us, she always had this outfit in a suitcase with her. It consisted of a nice black alpaca skirt, black silk taffeta waist with white ruching around the neck, and a new black cap with lace on it. There was also a new pair of slippers and stockings and a set of underwear. This was the kind of clothes she wore all her later life, and she wanted to be assured a "decent burial," and to cause no one any trouble when she died.

There were three other tastily furnished rooms off this bedroom —sitting room, parlor, and a bedroom opened only for much company. The parlor had a horsehair walnut settee, reed organ with peacock feathers in painted white glass vases on each side, center table with a fancy white doily that hung down on all sides. This held the large kerosene lamp with the painted globe and the sacred red plush album where Hans's picture was kept and wept over.

These rooms were used only when there was a lot of company. Otherwise, all the living, cooking, and eating took place in the big room which you first entered from the side door. It was a very pretty room. On the walls were two pictures, Currier and Ives prints, of a lady with a fan, and another with two doves. There was a clock shelf with lace scallops around it. This clock was of dark wood, and was rounding at the top. It had long since ceased to strike, but it did some very important other things; it could tell the day of the month as well as the hour and minute, and could tick loud enough to let you know it was there.

The floor of this room was shining varnished oak, covered with yards and yards of hit-and-miss rag rugs. The large oval dining-table was always set with sugar bowl, spoon holder, vinegar cruet and toothpick holder, with perhaps a fruit jar full of wilted flowers in the middle. Tone was so saving that she could never even throw flowers out until they hung limp along the sides of the jar. She could make a tiny fire in that stove of hers with a twisted piece of newspaper and a few chips which would make a pot of coffee, fry a few potatoes, and no more.

Along one wall was the carpet-covered lounge where Joseph sat or lay to read the paper. Above it hung a hinged rack for newspapers. Her special corner was between the couch and the stove, just at the door of her little bedroom. It held her small pine rocker, in which she had rocked my John and all her babies, padded with cushion and back rest in flowered material, with crocheted tidies over that. Above it was a corner book shelf with a glass door which John had made for her, where the Bibles and prayer books were kept. In the window sill beside it were her sewing basket and case of small steel-bowed spectacles which she seldom used. In this corner she pieced a quilt for every one of her grandchildren (about a dozen, anyway, of quilts) when she was in her eighties, and never used glasses at all to do it.

It was a sight to see her sit in that corner when the mail had come, and read the Norwegian newspaper. "See here," she would cry in Norwegian, weeping. "Here are a poor woman in Texas and two children burned up in a fire. Oh, God preserve them. . . ." (Sniff, sniff). "Oh, You Great Time! Here is where a man was riding along and a big stone rolled off the mountain and pushed him into the valley. . . . Oh, God preserve us . . . ." "*Nei, nei, nei!* Listen to this. . . ." And she would fasten her eyes on the entire household so that we all had to give attention. "Here is a man who had eight children and a bad woman got him away and they haven't been heard of for two years, and now he's found dead. Have you ever heard such trouble. . . . Oh-h-h, that poor woman! Left with eight little bits of ones. . . . That's the way I was left, with three little bits of ones . . . and my man dead. . . ." She would shuffle through the rest of the paper, snuffling and crying, and after it was all over, blow her nose loudly, look out the window and say, "The sun shines. Joseph, you must go and pick those apples over by the barn before the birds get them."

She remained stingy at the table until she died, that is, except when company came, when she would hustle Joseph down the steep cellar trap door for dry, yellow cheese she had long kept in a crock, sour sauce, a tiny pitcher of milk, and she would get out stale cookies from a tin box in her pantry. But she had such pretty dishes—thick glasses with diamonds all over the sides, red tablecloths with fringed napkins, a china set with small brown leaves and vines all over it. She would fry potatoes and the fish that Joseph kept her supplied with at all times from the near-by river. My children never liked to eat there, but she was the most hospitable person in the world, and you would no sooner come for a visit than she would hustle to that stove with her twisted newspaper and light a fire, and before you knew it, the table was set and you were eating. Right after that, she would tell you it was time to start home, before it got dark.

The first time Erna brought her John there to visit, Tone set the table as usual, and served some sour strawberry sauce. Tone loved John on sight, and wanted to honor him. But the poor boy, who was not brought up in a large family, and knew nothing of the tradition of eating what your elders set before you, shuddered to his toes after the first spoonful, and exclaimed, "This stuff's sour!"

Tone, whose ears never missed a thing, rose in alarm from her seat at the head of the table, and asked, "What was that?" We were all frozen in our seats, while Erna tramped on John's foot and explained to her grandmother in a stammer that strawberry sauce was ONE thing that this new husband of hers could not eat. Tone was all excited. She would send Joseph down cellar after some good *cherry* sauce that Annie Larsen had given her two summers ago. It was all we could do to keep her from it, and John was pressed to eat several of her stale cookies to make up for the lack.

In 1933, even though she was ninety-three years old, Tone looked just the same as she had forty years before, except that she was a little more shrunken. There were still those silken white loops of hair under the black lace cap, the cheeks as rosy and the eyes as blue and bright. Long ago, when her upper teeth had been pulled, she got a false plate, which heightened her young appearance. To be sure, these new teeth had to do business with one old long tusk in the bottom jaw, but even this became her. She had never been sick much in her whole life, and had never complained in any way, no matter how much she suffered. One time, when she was ninety years old, she went out in the early fall to the little outhouse behind the grape arbor at her home. As she was coming out, her foot was caught in the door, throwing her backwards, and twisting her foot at right angles with the leg. She uttered not a cry, but lay there for half an hour, knowing that Joseph was in the barn and would come to the house pretty soon. When he did come hustling along, moving very fast for him, crying, "Ma, Ma, what is the matter?", she replied, "Joseph, I have twisted my foot. Take hold of it and pull it back in place." He protested vigorously, and offered to get the doctor, but she forced him to take hold of it and pull until he had snapped it back in position. That ankle remained stiff from then on, but she never complained. If you ever brought a doctor to her, she would immediately announce: "You can't do anything for me. Go back."

She and Joseph lived with John and me during the last four or five winters she lived, but she insisted that they could keep house by themselves in summer. She loved my John better than anything else on earth to the very last, and often told me how she loved me, and praised me for standing his hasty temper, and taking care of him so well.

The winter she was ninety-three, we went down there to take care of them. One morning, she was combing her hair in a corner of the big kitchen, where there was a little mirror. As she finished, she stepped backward and caught that stiff heel in the edge of the linoleum and fell and broke her hip. This was the only time that anybody had ever heard Tone complain. She was got into bed and the doctor called, and her groans were terrible to hear; coming from so stout a character you knew she was really suffering. It did not last long. She died in twelve days, and was buried in the little churchyard beside the Winchester church.

COURTSHIP

I HAVE NOW TOLD you about my folks and my husband's folks, and all the old people from Norway. Now I am going back and tell you about the young folks and the fun they had in their youth, and their struggles in settling down.

There were no shows or circuses, or anything much to amuse young people in those days, so about the only thing we could do to have fun was to dance. And I mean dancing. The young people these days don't dance; they kick, and jump up and down. We danced.

There were some families that tried to introduce games, such as Snap-and-Ketchum, Spin the Platter, and another one called the Engagement Ring. It had a little verse that we sang in Norwegian:

> I have a ring
> I let it wander
> From one to another,
> And now it is tied
> And thrown away.

Some person had to stand in the middle and guess who had the ring. It was very much like Button, Button, Who's Got the Button?

Some soft boys liked to play Post Office, but I never cared about it; neither did the rest. Nothing came up to dancing. Mother did not approve of it, and Father told me that the only thing I ever did to grieve him was to go to these dances. Even though it made them sad, I could not resist, and besides I never could see the sin in it. Not the way we danced. Those square dances, waltzes, schottisches, hop waltzes, polkas (both runaway and heel-and-toe), and money-musk—they were all so much fun! I just loved to dance them all, but I did not have a chance at it very many years. I was married when only nineteen and a half, and that was the end of it. John was no dancer himself—we girls said he danced like a bear on its hind legs—and he had such a jealous disposition that he could not bear to see another man touch me. So in order to live in peace with him, I had to cut out the most fun I ever had in my life. Therefore, I will give a warning to any young person that happens to read this: Never marry anyone so entirely different in disposition. John was happy as long as I was by his side, but I missed my fun.

John was about five years older than I. One reason he was so against dancing was that he had been very wild himself up to the time he was nineteen. Tone was a very devout Christian and she prayed earnestly that he would give up his drinking and dancing. He loved her so much that he finally promised he would, and he never broke that promise. He never danced again, and we never had liquor in our house in all our lives. I was only sixteen, however, and he was over twenty when we started to go together, and you can see he was already past what I loved the best from the very start. My only salvation was that he went away to work on the log drive in the spring, and on the boat each summer with his Uncle Ole Oleson, and would not come back until the rivers froze over in the fall. I really had a fling while he was gone.

Sometimes when I forget how old I am, I wish some of those good old days were back again! I enjoyed everything so. Everything was fun. Women did not have to work half as hard as they do now, or worry about keeping up with the Joneses. Instead of having about twenty different outfits to wear, as they do now, we got along with a couple of calico dresses for everyday, and a next-best one for going to call on a neighbor, or to town to sell eggs and butter. If we had two others besides for church and parties, we considered it a great plenty. Some of those best dresses we put a lot of work on. Some had nine ruffles on the skirt. The waists were always rather plain and tight-fitting. Believe me, we had pretty shapes in those days, too, because we wore corsets even for everyday, and our figures did not spread as in these days. On these best dresses, we always had some sort of lace collar and pin. One time it was the style to wear a pretty handkerchief about the neck instead, pinned with some sort of fancy clasp.

We all wore our hair in bangs, and the rest of it would be parted in the middle, or combed straight back. No nice woman parted her hair on the side; it was considered "sporty." Almost until I married I wore my hair hanging down my back in two long braids. Then it got to be the style to wear it in a pug on the top of the head, which I adopted, feeling very much grown up.

We always made our clothes at home, and the men's everyday shirts and jackets besides. One of our biggest jobs every week was ironing, for besides all the men's heavy clothes, we had our own ruffled dresses and petticoats that were two or three yards wide, with plenty of ruffles and tucks on them. There were no ironing boards. We laid a thick blanket on the kitchen table, with a clean cloth over it, and ironed with sad irons heated on the wood stove. If it was a hot day, the sweat would really roll off our foreheads when we ironed.

For everyday we wore sunbonnets starched as stiff as boards, and we never went outside the door a step without one on, not even to the woodpile or pump. It was considered a disgrace to get tanned, and these sunbonnets kept our complexions as white and pink as a rose. To keep them even whiter and pinker, we used to rub ripe cucumber juice over our faces, necks, hands, and arms. Buttermilk was considered very good for this, too, and we used it every day. We cleaned our teeth by fishing out a stick of charcoal from the ashpit of the stove, and rubbing our teeth with it. This was followed by rubbing with a clean wet rag. Our teeth were never filled, and we often pulled them ourselves by wiggling the decayed ones until they were so loose that they could be pulled out with fingers or pliers. If they were too big for this, or got to aching too badly, of course we had to go to a dentist in some near-by town to relieve the misery. It was taken for granted that all old people were almost toothless. I never remember anyone having false teeth until quite a few years after I was married.

We never knew what it was to press woolen clothes in those days, and there were no dry cleaners. If a spot got on a dress, it was sponged off with water. After the dress was so old that it couldn't be worn for nice any more, it could be washed. Our best clothes were worn only for funerals, weddings, or church. Right after we got home, off they would come, be laid on the table, brushed thoroughly and hung up on nails with spools on them on the wall. Our hats would be put in hat boxes. The men's clothes were likewise brushed and folded in their original creases and laid in a big chest or trunk upstairs. Their hats would be brushed and hung up, with a cloth over them to keep them from getting dusty.

For a while we girls wore hoops, but they were too much of a nuisance for our active life. The center of gaiety for Sunday afternoon was the home of Halvor and Anne Johnson (Tone's brother and Torger's and Anne's oldest daughter). They had several children that were full of fun—Olena, John, Henry, and Serena, and two little tots named Elmer and Julia. Olena and Serena changed their names to Lena and Sarah as soon as they started to school.

On a summer Sunday afternoon, the Johnsons' entire front yard would be filled with young people, especially young men lying too thick to step between. And there would be quite a few girls on the porch and steps, giggling and tittering and flirting, answering the boys' teasing. No wonder everybody gathered there. Those days the farmers didn't have so many cows that we had to hurry home to help with the milking. So the young folks hung around when the sun got low, and they were never disappointed. The good-hearted Cousin Anne would get out bread and butter, applesauce, cake, and coffee, and even lemonade sometimes, which hardly anyone else had except on the Fourth of July. After it got dark, if there was no place else to go, the boys could at least walk the girls home.

Finally, I guess Halvor figured out a way to get those boys off his lawn. They had a nice grove of oaks just north of the house which they used as a picnic grounds. There Halvor erected a stout pole upon which he fastened a long timber with a swing at each end. These swings looked just like a window frame with a seat, in which the young folks sat and swung. You can believe it was fun to sit up there, one girl facing one way, another the other, and have some strong boys pushing the timber around and around like the wind, while the girls squealed with glee.

To get up into one of these seats, you stood with your back to it, took hold of the frame with two hands raised up by your head, and gave a little hop. At the same time you had to be quick as a wink to catch hold of the back of your hoop before you landed in the seat, or the whole front of your skirts and hoop would fly right up in the air, much to the amusement of bystanders. After a few such embarrassing accidents, we girls left off wearing hoops. Mother was glad. She burned mine up.

When the bustle craze came through our town, I was working and had money, so I bought one, because I always liked to be in style. It was a light thing of wire and cloth, about as big as a loaf cake. This contraption was tied under the petticoats with a couple of tapes that reached around the waist. The skirts fell over it in the back and gave you an exceedingly straight-front, curved-back look, which was supposed to be handsome, according to the fashion books. The old folks protested that it was a sin to distort the shape of the body like that, but we girls wouldn't listen—it was such fun to look like the pictures. Well, one day someone heard that in Chicago there was a baby born with a bustle on its back. "Now," our elders said, "will you listen? That is a warning from God." You can believe me, that put an end to bustle-wearing in our entire crowd.

For going to town to "trade," we wore our second-best clothes. There was a little country store at Winchester where we went most of the time. This served as a post office, too. The farmers would sell their eggs and butter in exchange for groceries, sugar, coffee, raisins, tobacco, and yeast cakes. That was about all they used that they did not raise themselves. On special occasions we would get extracts, baking powder, and whatever else was needed for making cakes, but soda was used for leavening in other foods, biscuits, Johnny cake, cookies, and doughnuts. Very few yeast cakes needed to be bought, because once we got a start, we made our own yeast and kept it going from week to week.

By THE TIME I was seventeen, I was a pretty good baker and cook, and had the honor of being asked to bake at two weddings. The first one was for our Irish neighbors, the Nesbitts. Jim was getting married. His bride was from New London, Wisconsin, about forty miles away. Ella was a cozy, rosy-cheeked, brown-eyed, dark-haired Irish girl. She wore a red worsted dress that evening and was very pretty, and they were very much in love. There had already been a Catholic wedding in her home town, so this was just the celebration at his home. I baked quite a few cakes, though, light ones and dark ones. His mother, Maggie, made some very good bread, and as the custom was in those days, there were always nice raised biscuits, made like bread except that we added sugar and shortening and sometimes dried currants. As I remember they had roast turkey and all that went with it, and tea, as the Irish very seldom drank coffee. Not the Nesbitts, anyway.

In the evening they had a dance, and was that ever a jolly bunch! Irish, all of them, only one other Norwegian girl besides myself. The groom could dance just one thing, and that was the square dance, and as he was feeling extra good that night, he wanted me to teach him the two-step schottische. At first I hesitated, but he insisted, saying, "Be Judas, Thurinie, just jerk me ar-round any old way!" I tried, but he was a poor pupil, and I soon gave up. Poor Jim—that was not the first time I had disappointed him. He was always trying to go with me, but although he was the best soul in the world, I could not do it. I was so glad now that he had such a lovely, pretty, easy-going girl. He just about carried her around on a sofa pillow, and then he had to lose her. She died quite young, and he never married again, and died before he got very old himself.

The other wedding where I was head baker was at my cousin Lena Johnson's, where the young folks used to gather and have so good a time on Sunday afternoons. This was a very big wedding. The couple was married in the church in the afternoon, and after that came to her home for the big wedding dinner and celebration.

It took us two or three days to bake enough cakes for this affair. Another girl helped me, but she said she would not take any of the blame if things went wrong, so it was up to me to go ahead. Oh, of all the cakes at this wedding! I guess they expected seventy or eighty people. We made white cakes, dark cakes, silver and gold cakes, chocolate and cocoanut cakes, maybe a couple of each kind. Layers and loaf cakes, too. The wedding cake was a three-tiered fruit cake, filled with all kinds of raisins and currants and maybe citron. The bottom was made in a good-sized, round milk-pan, the next a little smaller pan, and the top the smallest of all. It was a pretty, white-frosted cake, and good tasting. We had every-thing we wanted to do with, plenty of eggs, cream, butter, and milk in those days, for you could not get much for anything at the store, so we did not have to spare the ingredients. Then there was lovely bread and those good sweet raised biscuits with currants, shortening, and sugar in them. Halvor had butchered a calf for meat, and they had mashed potatoes, pickles of all kinds, and jelly; mince and apple pies, and coffee made in the washboiler. There was not another inch to spare on the tables for all the food. Luckily I was not responsible for all this food, just the cakes and cookies. And don't think any of us got paid for it. It was supposed to be a great honor, and it was. You had to have people you could trust and who knew their business when you had such an important event as a wedding.

Everybody for miles around was invited, of course. Mother felt insulted if anyone came on foot to invite her to a party or a wedding. She would say after they left, "I have been used to having people come on horseback with such invitations. People have no 'respect' any more." But she would go, so as not to hurt their feelings, just the same.

In those days the wedding would be at the church at 2 P.M., but the cook could not go. She had to stay home and prepare the big meal, so I was doubly glad that my work was over beforehand. The cook was a housekeeper for one of their neighbors, a very capable woman. They may have given her a little money for helping out.

A bride in those days didn't wear a veil. She would have a wreath of artificial flowers around her head, which matched the groom's buttonhole bouquet. His trousers would fit very tight, and the coat would probably have one button and be cut away in front. The bride's dress would be of worsted, since all weddings were in the fall, winter, or early spring. People were too busy in summer to fool around with celebrations.

The presents usually were rather simple, like a pretty picture, a bedspread, a set of six water glasses and pitcher to match. Some gave a little money, usually a dollar, and some a pretty dish.

The wedding supper was served some time after the couple came back from the church with all the guests. At this Johnson wedding, the table was set for fourteen to fifteen people. When it came time to eat, the bride and groom were seated first, then their attendants, then the minister and his wife, then the parents and closest relatives, until the first table was full. After they had eaten, it did not matter about the order of seating. There was always plenty to eat, no matter how many tables we had to set. Usually pretty young girls acted as waitresses.

After everyone was full and satisfied, the young folks would begin to look at each other, saying with their eyes, "Oh, I wish that minister would hurry up and go home so we can dance!" As a rule, he did not stay very late, and no sooner had he gone than the fiddler would go out and get his fiddle from his buggy or cutter, and sit down in the room where they were to dance. We could hardly wait until he could tune up his violin and begin the square dance, which was the custom as the first dance at a wedding. The bridal couple and attendants would make the first set. It took four couples for a set and in those days no one had more than two attendants, a sister of the groom and brother of the bride, if they had any, if not, they would have the next closest to both of them.

During the night, beer and whisky and wine were passed around a few times so that the fiddler could put more pep into the violin, and the dancers feel more light on their feet. Of course, not one of the girls ever put any kind of drink to her lips but homemade beer, which was so mild that you couldn't have got drunk on a gallon. The dance would last until two or three o'clock in the morning, when the guests would begin to leave.

There were no wedding trips in those days. The bride and groom would stay in her mother's house the first night and move to their new home the next day, or as soon as their new place was ready to start housekeeping. Those that had to move far off with their new husbands would stay at home a few days after the wedding before they said the sad farewell.

And so the weddings were celebrated in those days. Some married well and were happy ever after. Some did not and usually had to suffer for it later in life. If young people would think twice and weigh the matter carefully before they chose their mates for life, there would be fewer broken hearts and homes. I do not remember that there were many divorces in those days. If people made a mistake, they remembered their vow at the altar and stuck to it for the children's sake. I believe that Margit's daughter Anna and my husband's sister Julia were the only exceptions. People took more from each other those days, and made the best of a bad bargain if they got one.

When my children were growing up, I always told them to pick out good company. I told them not to marry anyone who was different in his ways and thoughts from them, because if they disagreed beforehand, they certainly couldn't agree afterwards. And I told them not to be in too much of a hurry. I can say that all my children have led nice, decent lives with their mates, even though some have been happier than others. There have been no divorces among my eight children, and I am thankful to God for all these blessings.

WHEN I WAS about sixteen or seventeen years old, it was time for me to go out and earn a little money. There was only one thing for the farm girls to do in those days, and that was housework. It was not the worst thing for a girl to go out and learn to do housework nicely, and it made good housekeepers out of us. I could go out to work only in the winter, for in the summers I was needed at home. I worked for different farm women and for relatives who needed help. We got from $1.50 to $2.00 a week. The last place I worked was in Winneconne for a very nice woman. No one ever abused me. I was like a member of the family wherever I went. This woman, in particular, taught me a lot about American housekeeping that my mother did not know. Another time I worked picking hops for the Allens in Allenville. Years later one of their sons defended us in a very important lawsuit that I will tell you about in another chapter.

This hop-picking was lots of fun. It lasted two weeks, and we got room and good board and worked with a group of young people all day, kidding and laughing. The hops grew on poles several feet apart. When the hops were ready to pick, there were young men who would pull up both poles and vines and bring them to where we were picking. These were called "box tenders." We girls picked the hops off the vines and put them into boxes, being paid by the box. We had a place to eat and sleep in a building attached to the house. Every single evening there was a dance in the hop

149

house. Since they dried the hops upstairs, not on the first floor of the hop house, the lower floor was empty. All the light we had was lanterns hanging around, but we didn't care. We could see to dance, and the fiddler played by ear. The dance would probably not last more than two or three hours.

Lots of well-to-do Norwegians and all the Yankees looked down on the girls who worked out. No Yankee girl ever did it. It was not until we were married and settled down that the working girls reaped their reward. Whereas the well-to-do, proud Norwegian girls, who had thought it a disgrace to be a servant, now kept house in their same old-fashioned ways, we others had learned all the nice, up-to-date American ways, and American cooking, and were not a bit sorry.

Sometimes it was not easy. Believe me, when my own girls were growing up, I worked my fingers to the bone to get them a good education so that they would have it easier than I did.

THE ONLY training I had outside of the little country school and parochial school, and in learning to do housework the American way, was a five week's course in dress-making in Neenah. One of my older sisters had already taught me to sew. At first we sewed everything by hand—dresses, shirts, jackets, everything—using a running stitch in the seams. When I was about fifteen, my sister Sena brought home a second-hand sewing machine, and that made sewing fun. When Sena would come home for vacations, she would sew for the whole family. Otherwise I did some of it even at an early age.

The person who taught this sewing course in Neenah was a Danish lady. Although she had a husband and a little girl, she kept a shop over a store right on the main street. You can believe it was lots of excitement for me to go to a town this big—three or four thousand people. A friend of mine, Elizabeth Madison, and I rented a room from a Danish widow there; we took along food from home and boarded ourselves.

Our night life was much duller than back in the country, however, as we did not know any young people. We were scared to death to venture out alone in such a big town. A couple of times we did go to see a friend from home, but aside from walking about a little when we were through with work, we stayed pretty close to our room. One time we heard that there was to be a masquerade in a dance hall and decided to take it in. We did not mask, of course, but went and looked on. No one asked us to dance, or paid any attention to us, so we finally went home.

The owner of the dress-making shop did not pay us for working from 8 A.M. to 5 P.M. each day. We had to pay her, in fact— five dollars for the model to cut patterns by. It was made of tin and cardboard and had little thumb-screws by which one adjusted it to proper size. All day long we helped this lady make dresses. After five weeks she told me that there was no need of my staying any longer, for I knew all she could teach me. Most pupils had to stay from three to six months before they were through. But I had been sewing under the direction of my big sister before this; that was why I caught on so quickly. That last week the lady taught me to take measurements of women who came into the shop to have dresses made, then to cut patterns from the model. I did not know then how very handy these lessons would be when I was married and became the mother of six girls. Tissue paper patterns were unknown.

As I SAID before, while I was doing all this, John was working on the river, logging and running his Uncle Ole's boat. He never wrote to me, and I was too busy to think of him much. But when he did come home, he just parked at our house so that I couldn't run out to dances. To tell the truth, the others boys were scared to death of him, because he was the strongest young man in the entire community, and he would have tackled anybody who dared to shine around his girl.

We had a good time there at home, when I could forget what fun the rest of them were having at the dance. John was always noted for his good story-telling, and he could keep a roomful of people interested. The tales of the logging days were so exciting that many people didn't believe him. But he never changed his stories throughout life, so I knew they were true. He said that once while working on the boat, he fell in the river with a long iron chain around his shoulders. John could never learn to swim, but he had such powerful muscles that he got out some way and came up with that chain. Nobody could ever understand how he did it.

I have told you how he fell in many times while walking along the slippery logs, and of how the Indians would rush to pick him out of the water. He could make friends with anybody. Years later, when we were living on the Waupaca farm and John was building cottages at the lakes, he had an Indian helper named Alec Parkhurst from the Keshena Reservation. Alec had been educated out East and was a wonderfully honest and trusted character. But he was an Indian still. When we asked him if he wanted to wash his hands before eating, he would say shortly, "Indian no wash." Remembering the Indian drifts we used to see in my childhood, at first I was inclined to be afraid of him, but when I got to know Alec, he was like a member of the family. He was devoted to John, especially, loved him as a dear friend, and worked for him nine years.

Another time John told the tale of a forest fire. It was while they were logging up in the woods. He said the flames came snapping through the pine trees like thunder and lightning. The only thing that saved the logging crew was a small river near by. They all rushed for it, and ducked themselves from the intense heat and reaching tongues of flame.

John told me, not once but a hundred times, that he had me picked out for his own since I was a mere child, and I did not know a thing about it except for occasional teasings that people did. We saw each other once in a while throughout childhood, but he didn't mean any more to me than the other boys.

It so happened that Uncle Ole Böe lived next farm to Tone's. He had these three girls that I loved, Signe, Gurina, and Anne. After I got to be about ten years old, I used to go over to Uncle's and help the girls pick mustard out of the grain fields. They had got hold of some seed oats that were full of this terrible weed. It took years to get rid of it in the fields. They would be so yellow with mustard blossoms that you could not see much else. Every summer, for a few years, it took two weeks to clear the fields of it.

One time when I was there, I had laid my sunbonnet on the ground. I suppose it was kind of cloudy just then, and I did not need it. When I went to put it on again, something cold ran around my neck. I thought it was a snake, and I ran yelling to the end of the field before I stopped. How my cousins laughed!

Well, this farm must have been the place where John saw me so much, but I don't remember talking with him before I was sixteen. That was the first time I had a little flirting with him, and we began to go together soon after that. But our courtship was not too good. I liked John, but I liked to dance better, and he could not stand to see me with another man. He did not care to dance at all by then, having sown his wild oats by the time he was twenty-one.

A young girl of sixteen is surely not ready to be an old woman. When he wouldn't go to parties, I sometimes accepted the invitations of other boys. Then he would be so mad at me that he would not look at me for months, but I did not care much. I was flattered by his attentions, and liked him for many reasons, though. He was very good looking, for one thing, of medium height, with heavy curling brown hair, and the prettiest blue eyes of anybody I ever knew. There was a sort of fire in them that burned into me even across a room, for they followed me everywhere. And he was about the most capable young man in the country. Whereas other boys around there earned a mere $12.00 to $15.00 a month working on farms, John made $60.00 clear a month working as engineer on Captain Ole Oleson's tugboat. I had a lot of my mother's and father's pride, and I thought I would have it pretty nice if I married John. He earned so much, and spent so little, I was sure he had a fine bank account.

So it went on for three and one-half years. We fought and made up, fought and made up, until he finally persuaded me to say I would settle down and get married. I wasn't half ready to, but he was a persistent person and was already twenty-four years old. My parents agreed to the match. The chief attraction for them was that, because his mother lived close by and the uncle for whom he worked was only eighteen miles away at Oshkosh, he would never take me far away, as the other sons-in-law had done to our older sisters.

I MADE MY own wedding dress. It was of brown wool sateen, they called it. The skirt was tucked across all the way down the front to a ruffle of box-pleats at the bottom. The top was a tight-fitting Polonaise, a sort of waist and overskirt in one, reaching almost to the ruffle in back, and as far as over the hips on the side. It was open in front to show off the tucks. At the neck I had ruching pinned together with a solid gold pin. It was a nice sort of diamond shape with spangles at the bottom, and had earrings to match, that my favorite sister, Sena, had given me one time. My shoes were high-buttoned black shoes, and I wore black stockings. Cotton, at that. Some style in those days, but whoever saw a woman's stockings anyway? My hair was drawn straight back and braided in two braids that were wound around the whole back of the head. The bangs were curled, and just above those rested a wreath of artificial flowers and green leaves. No bride wore a veil in those days. It was May 26, 1886, and the weather not very cold. I carried the wreath in a box, and for the wedding trip wore a brown straw hat trimmed with lace and flowers. Even though shawls were just about going out of style, I wore one instead of a coat. It was a sort of medium-brown Paisley with a fringe.

John had a black suit, tight in the trousers, and the coat was cut away sharply. He wore a white shirt with a stiff collar and a full-knotted black tie. In his buttonhole there was a bouquet of white artificial flowers to match mine (the regular bride-and-groom set) and his black shoes were buttoned.

It was on Wednesday morning, the twenty-sixth, that John called for me with a double-seated open buggy and a team of medium-weight farm horses. This particular buggy had a lot of sentiment attached to it. When my sister Anguline was married years before, Sam, her husband, had borrowed it from John Anunson, a neighbor, and they had driven to the church with their witnesses in it. My John had bought this buggy some time before our marriage from the Anunson family, and now here it came to take the second Kjeldalen girl to her marriage. My mother and Lena wept when we left. I can tell you I was not very gay when we pulled away from that old home place, and I realized I was leaving it forever.

John drove me back by his mother's place to pick up the witnesses. They were his sister, Julia, and his cousin, Charlie Barstad (brother to the famous Barney), who was working at their place just then. It took us a couple of hours to drive the eighteen miles to Oshkosh, and we went straight to the home of John's Uncle Martin Oleson. John had not told them a thing about it, and they were astonished when they heard the news. His Aunt Hattie was a cute little woman, so full of fun and hospitality, and such an excellent housekeeper. She exclaimed, "Well, I wondered when I saw you, what all these new clothes meant." We were going right over to the minister's house for the ceremony, but she insisted on us staying for dinner. She was a wonderful cook, but I may be excused if I forgot what we had to eat on that exciting day. All I can remember was the strawberries and cream, and that was a treat so early in the season. I suppose they had been shipped in. Uncle Martin was on his boat at the time, but he always saw to it that they lived well.

Aunt Hattie wouldn't hear to it that we should go to the parsonage to be married. She sent John for the minister, who came and married us right at her house. This man was a heavily-bearded person, the Reverend Mr. Wald, who preached in John's church in Winchester. We did not want to be married up there because we belonged to different congregations, and the fight was still on between them. This Wald had a church in Oshkosh, too, having moved there from Winchester so that his children might have better schooling. He was very surprised to see us, too, but he was a kind of old fogy and didn't have much to say. How I wished we might have had my good old Pastor Homme, but the very mention of it would have sent Tone right through the ceiling.

I thought it was nice that we were married in Oshkosh, anyway. That had always been John's headquarters in summer, with his uncle, Captain Ole Oleson, and I was sure that that was where we would live, and I was excited over the prospect. I always loved to be where things were going on, and Oshkosh was a lovely city.

John put on my finger that day a broad gold band that I have worn every day since, except when I worked in the garden and was afraid it would be lost. It is as bright and good as ever. Many couples of those days had their pictures taken soon after the wedding. But John wouldn't go. He hated picture-taking all his life, and I couldn't see why, for he was really handsome and took good ones. It was four months before I could persuade him to do it. By this time he had given me the prettiest present of his life. It was a heavy solid gold chain about one-half inch wide, with little links that were turned on their sides, so that the round part was on top. At the end of the chain was a small fat locket, decorated in blue enamel, which opened up to hold two small pictures. I always thought it set off my outfit very well in the picture. I shall tell you something interesting that happened about that picture when we come to the chapter on our golden wedding.

CHILDREN

EVEN IF IT HAD been the style to take a wedding trip in those days, I am sure John would have just taken me on that nice long ride in the double-seated buggy back to Tone's farm. As the days wore on, and we did not get back to John's job in Oshkosh, I began to inquire. Then he had to confess that we could not go that summer. Joseph had agreed to build a barn for Ole Leifson, his brother-in-law, and John would have to stay on the home place to help his mother.

After a while I found out that there was another reason. For all the money that he had earned since he was nineteen years old, he did not have a penny. He had given it all to his mother, who had put it into the farm, and there it was tied up. He had even had to borrow money from Charlie Barstad to get married on. It was pretty disappointing for me as a young bride to see my mother-in-law put first. John worked from dawn till dusk all that summer, and I never sat down while there was work to do in the house, but we got nothing for it but board and lodging. This went on for a whole year.

Tone's ways were so different from ours at home, that I could not be happy with her. She had had to struggle for herself so long that she had forgotten what it was to set a good table. I remember how I amazed her the first time I baked bread, after having made some good homemade hop yeast. Tone just could not make a good loaf of bread, and when I offered to do it, she was glad enough to let me try. Whereas her loaves were about three inches thick, and as heavy as lead, these hop-yeast loaves could hardly be got out of the oven, they rose so high. How my John enjoyed this bread! To the end of his days, he would say, "I would rather have your bread than cake." I baked an average of eight loaves a week for him for fifty-five years. You can figure how many that would be. I loved to bake bread.

I want to say here, though, that Tone and I never had a cross word in all our lives, despite all our differences in disposition and ways. At first, she was not pleased with the marriage, but as time went on, she began to warm up. She began to tell me how thankful she was that her hasty John had married a woman with patience. I do not consider this patience entirely good. If I had had a little more spunk at the very first, it would have been better for us both all through life.

I never quarrelled with John, either, or anyone that I remember. This love of peace I had inherited from my father. He never had an enemy in this world. Unlike him, however, when I'd had too much, I did give people a piece of my mind; but I didn't quarrel.

It wasn't long after our marriage that I found out John's two terrible faults. One was that he was never happy unless he was property poor, and the other was that he had an ungovernable temper. He did not get mad at people so much as at things that went wrong. Then the words he would say would make the air blue, and his eyes would send out flashes like hot darts from under his down-hanging brows.

I learned early in our married life that the best way to handle him during these spells was to act as if I never even noticed them. I would go about my work quietly and see that the meals were on time, though I very much doubt if he knew what he was eating. He appreciated my patience, and said so many times after the spells were over. He told our children once in later years that he had learned to throw these fits of temper while driving oxen in his youth. These animals were so stubborn that they sometimes would not obey ordinary commands. You've heard the saying, "stubborn as an ox." Well, it's all too true. Sometimes one could holler "Gee" and "Haw" and "Giddap" until he was hoarse, and they would just stand there. But if one swore real loud at them, and cursed them up and down, they would be very docile and do anything they were asked.

John's temper fits lessened greatly in his old age, and he asked one of the children in confidence once, "Have you noticed that I don't swear any more?" He knew it was a sin, and was so happy that he had broken himself of the habit.

These spells did not ever last long. If nobody opposed him, he would go storming out of the house, but in a little while be back again, as sweet as candy, with maybe a hatful of eggs as a peace-offering, and a great big kiss on the cheek for me.

I did not mind the tempers nearly as much as the sullen pouting that would last for three days. Then he would sit with his elbows on the table, chin in hands, staring fiercely out the window. Occasionally he would give a snort. I treated these just as I did the other spells, and the only time I spoke to him was when the meals were ready. These spells would be broken usually by the arrival of company, when he would be forced to be pleasant. He was one man that never wanted anyone to know that we ever had trouble, and would always face a stranger with a smile. By the time the company had gone, the spell was over, and we could all breathe again.

I guess no one in the family could have stood all this if it had not been for the fact that in between times he was one of the most light-hearted persons in the world. He always collected new jokes or told the old ones over and over, getting a new chuckle out of them each time, and laughing until the tears rolled down his cheeks. He loved to have fun with the children and could play with them like a kid himself, turning them upside down to let them walk on the ceiling, making telescopes out of his hands to peer at them if he were surprised, trotting them on his knee. Outsiders used to remark that we were the happiest family they had ever seen, because he never threw a fit in front of strangers.

We stayed on the farm all that summer and the next winter. On the third of March, my first baby was born. It was a stillbirth, and the child was buried the next day, on John's birthday. He felt crushed about it, because he was the tenderest-hearted father I ever knew. I saw him weeping, with his head between his hands, even over this one that never saw life. I had only one glimpse of the baby, when they brought the coffin to the bed. It was such a pretty thing, round and fat, but still and white as wax. I am happy to say here that this was the end of our bad luck with babies. All the other eight were strong and healthy and gave us much joy through the years.

That spring John once more went to work with his Uncle Ole on his boat in northern Wisconsin. I went home to my mother and stayed until he came back and got me. The next few months were some of the happiest we ever spent together. Ole's boat was anchored a mile away from Three Lakes, which was a great tourist center. They were through with their big logging drive, and had only an occasional job with the tugboat "Erna," which had been named after Ole's only daughter. All John had to do was to take care of the boat and rent out some row boats to the tourists. All I had to do was cook for John and me.

The tugboat was anchored near a big log tourist hotel, but the season's rush was over when I got there. The proprietor, a Mrs. Lee, and I had much fun, visiting and playing with her two little children. John used to take us for rides in a rowboat, and it was very cool and pleasant, rowing up and down the tree-lined banks.

WITH THE money he earned that summer, we bought our furniture and settled down in two rooms over a grocery store in Oshkosh. I was just beside myself with joy in this first home of ours, with all our own things, and being my own boss. These rooms were very large; one served as a kitchen and dining room, and the other as a bedroom and living room. John was an excellent carpenter, so he had no trouble finding work. Besides, he had this wonderful Uncle Ole to back him, whose name was magic in Oshkosh.

For the kitchen, John made me a nice cupboard, with two glass doors over the upper dish compartment, and two plain ones at the bottom where I kept the food and supplies. My stove was the pride and joy of that room. It was brand new and I kept it shining. There was a reservoir for heating cistern water in the back, and a warming oven below. It was what Norwegians called a "box stove." The oven was below the surface and had two doors. In the center of each door was a yellow porcelain disk about as big as a saucer, with the raised design of a goat. Of course, with oven doors so low, you have to watch children. The reason I know is that my oldest daughter, Clara, when she was about three, put her sister's shoes in that oven, and I hunted all over for them. The next time we had a hot fire in the stove, I learned where they were—in the oven, baked to a crisp.

All kinds of cooking utensils came free with our stove. A big round-bottomed iron kettle with short legs on it, iron frying pan, tin coffee pot, bread, cake, and pie tins, tin dish pan, tin steamer to set over the iron kettle for dumplings and puddings, tin teapot, tin stirring spoon, and best of all a big shining nickle-plated teakettle for hot water to scald the dishes. I must not forget the covered tin washboiler with copper bottom that was also thrown in free. The whole outfit, stove and all, cost twenty-six dollars.

I kept that stove for twenty-one years and it was just as good as the day I bought it. Then I was foolish enough, just for style, to trade it in for a great big Monarch malleable iron range. This stove cost eighty dollars, and they gave me only seven dollars for my old one in trade. The new one did not bake one bit better—hardly as good. And it took things much longer to get to cooking on the top because the firebox was so deep. The thing that took my eye was a wonderful modern heat indicator on the front of the oven. This would put an end to placing a piece of paper in the oven to see how brown it got in so many minutes, or putting in my hand and counting how many minutes I could stand it there. But to my great disappointment, this indicator never told the truth. I had it a long time before I discovered that its hand was put on backward.

Many times I wished for my old box stove with the yellow goats on it, but I had to be in style. This is an example of the many foolish things we do just for pride—casting off the old for the new when the old is the best. Many marriages would be saved if people would realize this truth.

In those days we could get plenty of pine slabs for fuel. It was only $1.50 a big load, as there was so much of that at the sawmills in Oshkosh. Our woodshed was the only upstairs woodshed I ever saw. It was just a few steps down to a platform that led to another building behind the store. This is where we kept our washtubs, bench, mops. John made me a great big box for storage out there. Since this was the "big town," we kept the woodshed door locked at night.

John was very thin when we married, not over 140 pounds. But as soon as we got by ourselves, he began to get fat. He just stuffed on my cooking. One of the first cakes of dry yeast I bought had a coupon on it, with which you could get a cookbook for twelve cents. I thought it would be a pamphlet, but to my amazement when it came it had three or four hundred pages, and such wonderful recipes. I tried every one in the book that I could afford.

John was very appreciative at table all our lives and learned to eat many things he would never touch before. You can believe he kept getting fatter and fatter, until he weighed two hundred pounds.

The yeast cakes that advertised this book were little round ones, six to a package, and they made the best bread, and other things from the book. It was a veritable Sears Roebuck catalog of a book. It was my guide in etiquette and how to behave like a lady in company, how to raise children, how to take care of clothes. I learned from it to put up gallons of the best mincemeat, all kinds of preserves and meats, cakes, salads, vegetables. I had to be prepared at all times for company, for we often had a lot of Winchesters drop in for dinner when they came to shop. Most of these were our dear relatives and friends, but some were just spongers that I didn't care a snap for. They came just to eat dinner, as it was considered very extravagant to buy a meal in a restaurant if you knew anyone who would give it free.

I hung my washing in a storeroom back of the store. John was always making something nice for me. He made a bench that we used all our married life, to set the water pail on in the kitchen. On washdays it was used for the tubs. Now for the first time in our lives we did not have to have our washdish on a bench. This wonderful convenient modern apartment had what everybody called a "zink" in the corner by the stove. It had a drain and a cistern pump from which I could use water for everything but drinking and cooking. This made it very convenient for John, who had to carry up the drinking water from a pump in the yard, and would have had to carry the waste water down if it had not been for that drain. All his life John was very good to me about lifting and helping me with heavy things, and nothing made him angrier than seeing me do heavy work that he could do. About the only fault that he found with me was that I worked too hard, especially cleaning. He would often liken me to Signe Böe Lee: "Sena says she'd rather be a little bit sick and clean, than healthy and dirty." That statement used to make him so mad, although he was very fond of Sena.

Our first bed was the one we used almost all our lives. It was an oversized one of solid walnut, with a very high headboard in various panels that went lengthwise of it. At the very top it was arched, and in the middle was a beautifully carved S. Uncle Ole Oleson had got us this bed, and we always wondered if it was from the rich Sawyers, it was such a fine piece of furniture. The footboard was about waist high and was gracefully arched like the top, and the ends bowed around to the side. With this bed came a marble-topped washstand, which had a drawer and two doors below. The carved drawer pulls were in the shape of cupped oak leaves.

To round out this set, my folks gave me as a wedding gift a walnut dresser, with a tilting mirror and two little drawers on top. There were three big drawers below. In those days hardly any of our folks had clothes closets. So my handy John made me a wardrobe to keep our clothes in. We had a new wooden rocker with arms and a high back, which I padded with pretty flowered cloth and cotton padding. Over the back rest I hung a big square crocheted tidy in rose design. I covered a feather cushion with the same flowered material.

My pride and joy was the new Singer sewing machine, because I not only loved to sew but had to keep us all in clothes. This I kept in the big bedroom-living room, too, for there was a new wood heater in there that I kept going all the time. When I went to the Singer office to order my machine, they immediately brought it up for me to try out. The New Home Sewing Machine Company got wind of this, and they also brought a machine right up there for me to try. The two agents raced up and down our steps all the time, knocking each other in every way, and even coming down on their prices, from forty dollars to thirty-five. I really liked the New Home the best, but my husband and his Uncle Ole said the Singer was the most dependable, so as usual I gave in. They were not mistaken. That old machine is still going strong. It sews as well today as it ever did, but has lost a lot of its nice looks, as everything else does when it gets old and worn.

Our first table is still in the family. It is of solid walnut with two drop leaves and two extension leaves. It had fluted and ball legs with white china casters. There is an interesting story about this table. By the time we had moved to the Waupaca farm, we had long since discarded this table for a shiny new oak dining table which had many extensions to accommodate our big family and our friends. The finish on the old table was pretty badly battered, since it had been used as a kitchen table for years, and at one time one of the children had painted it green. Finally it made its way to the milkhouse by the barn, and we used it to wash the milk utensils on. The summer after my daughter Erna was married, she came home to gather up her belongings so that she and her John could start housekeeping. She was washing the cream separator for me one day out in the milk house, when she happened to stoop and notice those fluted legs.

Coming into the house, she asked me what table that was. I replied, "Oh, that's just the old table I started housekeeping with."

"What kind of wood is it?" she asked.

"Walnut, I guess," I replied.

"Walnut!" She nearly went wild with joy, and begged me for it on the spot. The antique craze was just coming in. It took her and John six weeks to scrape all that old finish down to the wood and to restore its finish as when it was new. I have to laugh when I see it now under an antique walnut mirror in her living room. I suppose her daughter will be crazy over golden oak.

While we were setting up housekeeping in those first two rooms, my husband happened to go to a jewelry store auction, and bought me as a surprise a very fine walnut eight-day Gilbert clock. It was covered with pretty carving, with pointed spindles on the sides and a carved angel at the top. The pendulum was of bright nontarnishable gold-colored metal, round, with a curved stem and leaf at each side. This swung back and forth in front of a round space in a spider web frosted on the arched glass door. It had a beautiful chime. My daughter Clara has it now, and it still keeps good time.

John made a shelf for this clock, and I crocheted some yellowish-brown scallops, with two rows of insertion, into which I wove two rows of red ribbon, with a bow. By this time, however, I was citified enough to call it a "lambrequin."

EVEN WITH ALL this buying, we had saved two hundred dollars by the next year, and used it as a down payment on Uncle Martin's house, where we had been married. It was almost a new house, and such a solid one, having been built by a good German contractor named Euiler. It still stands on Bowen Street, and I wish I had it now. There were five rooms and a pantry, a new woodshed, cellar under the whole house with a great cistern in it, running water in the kitchen, and best of all, a closet in the front bedroom. Coming from the little log house where I was brought up, you can imagine that I thought I lived in a mansion.

We had one dear little boy by this time, Harry, and kept on having children, one about every two years. I never minded the work because I was so happy with the children, and it was such fun to be the mistress of my own house, for until this time I had always been bossed by either John's or my own mother. I even took in boarders, and in a few years we had paid up the whole $1,250.00 that the house cost.

John still made good money steadily, winter and summer. Captain Ole Oleson had got him a job as engineer in the water works in Oshkosh. It paid well, $60.00 a month, but John became restless. There was too much *sitting* to this job, and he got awfully fat. He yearned for activity for those strong muscles of his. After a few years, he quit and went back to carpenter work. There was not as much money in it, but it suited him better.

It was John's terrible fault that he could never let well enough alone. If we ever got settled nicely in some place, as sure as anything, he would buy another piece of property and get us in debt. There was one time when we had four places, and were in debt on three of them.

While he was remodeling a house out in the country, he noticed a nice ten-acre piece of land for sale, half a mile outside of the city limits. Nothing must do but he must have this, and paid $1,800.00 for the land alone. Then he sold our little home on Bowen Street and built an enormous ten-room house out there, with two stairways, six bedrooms, and closets all over the place. It had an enormous porch across the front, one on the back, and a big woodshed. John was never satisfied if he didn't have a nice house to live in, the bigger the better. He also put up a barn with a cupola, a large chicken coop, and a corncrib. He set out all kinds of apple trees and berry bushes, grape vines, and strawberry beds. John still kept his carpenter job in town and worked this land in his spare time, after supper and before breakfast. No one could ever accuse him of being lazy.

This was the first time that the work got too much for me. We had four children when we moved there, and soon had two more. If the older ones hadn't helped to take care of the little ones, I couldn't have kept on. When the berries got ripe, the work was really driving. Every afternoon I had to start to pick raspberries and fill the crates which stood in the shade. When John got home, he would carry the crates down cellar to keep cool until the next day, when he would take them to town as he drove back to work.

One year we had a strawberry crop that was the awfullest yield of strawberries I ever saw. The summer we had set them out, I hoed the entire patch seven times. In the fall, John covered the whole field with horse manure. By the next year, when the crop was ready, I had just had another child, Erna, and got out of picking berries that year. So we had to hire pickers by the dozen, and a man to sell them. Our profit from this was only four cents a box, and yet we cleared over $100.00 and gave away crates and crates of them to relatives and friends.

We had one exciting night at this Ten Acre place. One time our next neighbor's house caught fire in the night. It had got such a start before anyone noticed it that it burned to the ground. We lived so close to that house that we frantically got all the children out of bed and downstairs. Some of them still talk of being held in John's strong arms as he took them down the steps, and of seeing that patch of red flame in the stairway window. The roof of our house did catch on fire from the flying sparks, but John and some neighbor men got it out before damage was done.

Harry was able to run down stairs himself, of course, and the darling thought first of all of the big family Bible that Tone had given us, which laid on the center table in the front room. Without asking anyone, he ran in and got it, and lugged the heavy book to the neighbor's fence on the other side, and covered it with leaves. We were all so touched when we found out the next morning what he had done.

Though the work was hard here, we loved this Ten Acres, and we love to go by the place now to see the old house that John built. There was plenty of space for the children to play, and my children were always healthy, with cheeks like red apples and shining blue eyes. The first four children had dark brown hair. My hair by this time was turning from red to dark brown all the time, and I was very glad each time a child was born that none of them had that disgraceful color, red, that I had been teased so much about in my childhood.

Our children all had such different characteristics, but all were so sweet and smart that John and I were foolish over them. Harry was the light-hearted, happy-go-lucky one, with mischievous eyes. He was a tinkerer from the time he could hold a tiny hammer. When he was only ten years old he fixed up his wagon for the mastiff that his Aunt Julia had given him. This Prince was a huge, powerful dog, brindle in color, whose head came almost to my hips. Harry put thills on his play express wagon, and a bowed top like a covered wagon. It was no trouble at all for this dog to draw the wagon with several children squealing with joy inside it.

Later on Harry took to making violins, the first one out of a cigar-box. After a while he made a real violin, gluing and shaping and varnishing it in his father's workshop. He could make bows and arrows, sleds, and skis. Then later he took to drawing and painting with oils. John and Tone were so crazy about this boy that they spoiled him, and let him do anything he wanted. Pretty soon, he wanted to quit school, and then we couldn't do anything with him. Captain Ole Oleson was still alive then, and I know that he would have helped get that boy to West Point, for he had much political influence in Wisconsin. But Harry would not go farther than second year high school.

Our next child was a girl whom we christened Clara Tonetta. It was the old Norwegian custom that you should name your babies after relatives, but it wasn't always followed. They were just as proud if you gave the child a name that began with their initial. You can see that Tonetta had Tone's name in it, and the "T" stood for Thorild, too. Harry's middle name was Martinius, with the initial "M" after my father, Mathis, and the Harry after John's father, Hans. People would have laughed at us if we had named our child Hans Mathis, so we got as close to it as we could.

Nearly all my children were christened in the same long robe, for which Tone had given me the cloth. It had an organdy yoke, but the skirt was all-over lace. Beneath it, the poor babies had to wear two other long petticoats. The under one was of fine white wool flannel, and the upper of heavy white cloth with embroidery at the bottom. After I'd used it for seven children, I thought I was through, and used that skirt to cover a parasol that was attached to the baby buggy. The last child had to have a new christening robe.

Clara was born sober, and because she was the oldest girl, felt a great responsibility for the younger children. I always had so much to do that she had to take care of them. Clara was the only one that had as heavy hair as mine. It was dark brown and I kept it in two long braids down her back. This was so cute, because she was small, and yet so smart and important. By the time she was eight, there was no more playing with dolls, but we would find her every free moment with a book. She would be absolutely gone and lost—we could hardly make her hear when she got interested in a book. I would often find her rocking a baby, shaking it in the crook of one arm, and the other hand had the open book.

Stella had music in her fingers and in her voice and steps from the time she was born. When she was six months old I used to lay her on a cot by the window where a poplar tree grew outside. Now, the leaves of a poplar tree twist and turn in the wind all the time, and as she lay there, she would turn her little hands with them, and laugh and kick until she almost wiggled herself off the bed. Nothing ever bothered Stella much as she was growing up. Everything was a lark for her. She was the only one of my children that had curly hair like John's. I could curl it on my finger, and it would stay that way all day.

Early in life Stella began to mother and nurse everybody in the house. When she was just tiny, I was lying on the cot one day with a headache. Before I knew it, here came Stella with a wet napkin and laid it across my forehead. She was always so willing, and on the trot doing something for someone. To the little sisters and brothers that came along, she was a mother, fussing and fixing their hair and clothes, taking them on picnics, reading and playing and singing to them. In school she always had a beau, and either he or she would be sent to the cloakroom every so often for passing notes.

My children were all pretty smart in learning music, but I never did like an organ. When they got old enough to take lessons, I looked around Oshkosh until I found a fine old-fashioned square piano. It was of mahogany, with a lovely carved music-rack. It was very large and long, with huge round legs paneled down the sides. John was just as happy to get this piano as I. We paid only $60.00 for it, and were the first ones in our whole relationship to have one. Harry and Clara started to take lessons, but Harry didn't last long. That was too confining for him. He had to be out shooting with the new air-rifle that his father had given him. But Clara stuck faithfully to it, and then Stella began to take lessons. She was so crazy about it that I never had to make her practice, and she learned trills and runs in her pieces that made John and me stand back and smile with pride. There was a Mrs. O'Dell from Butte des Morts who drove around the country giving lessons for thirty-five cents apiece. We got a bargain because there were two—fifty cents for both. Both girls learned to play for their schoolrooms and hymns for Sunday School.

I have told you how John loved the children. One time Stella took a notion she wanted a skirt with shoulder straps, to go with a pretty waist I had made her. Since I had one of my numerous babies at the time, I asked John to select some sort of nice plaid material about fifty cents a yard, which would have been a high price in those days. Yes, he got plaid, all right, at ninety cents a yard! It had a white and black silk stripe on a bright red background, and I had orders from him to make it into pleats. John had one idea for women's clothes: pleated skirts. When I was over sixty years old, and they had gone completely out of style, he so nagged me about them, that I had to make one of black silk. Every time he saw it, he would lean back and admire it. This red plaid dress of Stella's really saw its day. The cloth never wore out, or got dingy, no matter how much it was used. For years and years it was made over for the little girls, and it finally ended up in a crazy quilt that one of them got when she was married. Like his father, John never wanted anything cheap.

I loved to sew for my girls. When I went to town, if I saw a pretty remnant, I would buy it, whether I needed it then or not. And I always would pick up the fashion plates beside the door of the store. When I got home, I would sit down in a small rocker and gather the girls about me. "Now, pick out the way you want your dresses made," I would say. One would want this, and the other would want that. Of course, the older ones' dresses would be cut down again and again for the younger ones. That was harder work than making new. It took all my spare time to keep my daughters dressed nicely. I never had time to gad around through the week. In the spring and fall I used to sit up until ten at night. There was a little blue kerosene lamp with a handle that just fitted on the back of my sewing machine, and the light fell just right on the sewing so that I could see as well as in daylight. I did the cutting and fitting and basting during the day, but saved all the stitching until night.

In the winter, I had to catch up with the spring sewing and the odd jobs, like making quilts, rugs, and so forth. It was lucky that in those days sisters dressed alike, so it was easier for me, since I had two pairs of girls about the same size. For years and years, middy suits were popular, and I could make them when the girls were away at school. With these, of course, would go John's favorite pleated skirts, which did not require much fitting, either.

Our fifth child was a boy, as sober as a deacon, and very independent from babyhood. One time when we lived on the Ten Acres, and he was only four years old, I was talking with a neighbor at the back fence. Presently I glimpsed Emil coming to the house from the road with a large package in his arms, and just then the travelling butcher wagon drove off. I asked Emil what in the world he had in his arms. He replied: "I went down cellar and looked in your meat barrel, and saw it was empty. So I bought a soupbone." It was almost as big as he was.

"Where did you get the money?" I asked.

"Oh, I went into your pocket book and found two white pennies." He was so crazy for soup, that he provided for it; he has been like that all his life.

Then he began to tease for a pony. One day when he and John were driving along the road, they met a man with two mother Shetland ponies and two colts. He stood up in the rig and pointed, crying, "There, Pa—there, Pa, there's my pony!" Good old John! He ordered the man to come to the farm the next day with the pony. He had to get Emil a saddle, of course, and then a cowboy suit and a riding whip. The boy would go galloping around the country, although he was just six years old, stopping in to see all the relatives, where he would be sure of a cookie and maybe a drink of milk.

Emil rode Daisy until his feet nearly dragged on the ground when he was on her back. Then we got him a rubber-tired cart, which the girls could use, too. One day when Clara was driving the cart, Daisy stopped right on the railroad track and got caught in the gates with the train coming. Clara screamed and the gate man noticed her and raised the gates in time. This frightened us so, especially since Daisy now took to holding the bit in her teeth and running away, that we sold her. It nearly broke the children's hearts, the little ones who used to feed her lump sugar and handsful of clover. We traded her and a horse named Pearl and our big piano for a new upright oak piano that the big girls had been teasing for.

Erna was our sixth child. She was the first real blonde, and had the fine skin that went with it. She could color up like a strawberry if a stranger noticed her, and was so timid all through her childhood that she would climb a tree with a book and some apples when company came. She and I were dear friends from the very first—she was such a Mama baby. One time when she was four years old, Albert Hough, a neighbor, came along and saw her standing by the gate. "Well," he asked, "how old are you?"

Erna looked up at him with a smile and said gravely, "Six-*teen*."

Now the two older girls and two older boys were always together, leaving Erna alone. Maybe that's why she clung to me so much. But when she was a little over two years old, they led her into my bedroom, showed her a new baby and said, "Here's a sister for *you.*" We called the new baby, Henrietta, after her grandfather Hans (or Henry as he called it in English). She was the healthiest and spunkiest of all my children, and had a tongue as quick as an Irishman's. She was so pretty and cute that everybody noticed her wherever she went. She and Erna were inseparable. They would climb trees together, go fishing, play paper dolls, read or work, anything, just so they could be together.

The moment Ida was born I felt that she looked like Kristine. I could never feel easy about this child, she was just too angelic. Whereas the other children would fight and tussle and scream and yell, Ida was always quiet and peaceful. I can never remember having to discipline her. When she was old enough, she went to kindergarten and learned a little song, which she would skip around singing, with her flaxen hair bobbing up and down on her back:

> Pretty little blue-bird, why do you go?
> Come back, come back to me-ee.
> "I go," said the bird, as he flew up high,
> "To see if my color will match with the sky."

When Father, at the age of ninety-three, was taken in his last illness, they called for me to come home. I went, taking Thelma, the baby, with Erna as nursemaid. Ida and Henrietta were left in care of their father and the big girls, because it was Christmas vacation. After two weeks I got a letter that the little girls had a bad cold, and that I should come home. It was terrible for me to leave my dying father, who called for me every day, and whom I knew I would never see again. But my own family had to come first. When I got home, Ida was very sick. We called the doctor, but by this time it was discovered that she had whooping cough and double pneumonia. It would have been hard to save her even today, and surely not by the crazy methods they used then. I do not know what kind of doctor this man pretended to be, but he would only let me give her whipped egg-white. One day she asked for a banana, and I gave it to her. This made the doctor angry.

John was almost wild as he saw how things were going with the child. He came in and asked her what on earth he could give her to while away the time in bed. She asked for a "big dollie, with golden hair and blue eyes and a pink silk dress." One of the big girls was dispatched to town to get it for her, and we dressed it as she had ordered. She was too weak to hold it then, but she braced it against her knees, and named it "Stella," for the big sister who had always tended her so lovingly. She lived only ten days after I came home, and then early one morning she died. This was the worst blow that I had ever had in my life, and I thought it would kill me. She had died the day after Father's funeral, so I had double sorrow. I could never stand the house in which we lived after that, so John moved us over a store he had built. There we lived for three years.

I was nearly forty years old when Thelma was born, so she was the comfort of my old age when all the rest of the children were gone. I was not very well throughout her childhood and do not know what I should have done but for Erna. Being the baby, Thelma, of course, was spoiled. There were times when only Erna could handle her. She took her with her everywhere she went, amused her, trained her, and loved her. When Erna and Henrietta had to go away to high school, poor Thelma was left alone, and then she turned to the dog for comfort. We had at that time a fine big collie-and-shepherd dog, named Taylor, who shared all her joys and sorrows like a playmate.

I remember the first time an airplane went over our farm. John and I were in the house, but Thelma had gone down to the pasture, about a mile away, to get the cows with Taylor. As we waited there for her return, a rumbling and buzzing appeared in the sky. We looked at each other in amazement, and then John cried, "Ma, it's an airplane!" None had ever flown over our place before, and we had never seen one. But our joy at seeing it was dimmed because Thelma wasn't there. When she came home, we both said, "An airplane went over our house. Did you see it?"

Thelma was so excited that she swelled up instead of answering. Finally she burst out, "You b-b-bet I DID!" That was just like her; she never missed anything.

John's devotion to the children and to me showed itself over and over again throughout life. He could almost never eat a dessert, but would pass it over to some shameless child who knew that a tender look that way would make him yield it gladly. I used to scold them for letting on they wanted another dish of dessert, because John would as sure as anything give up his. I used to see him planning and thinking for them, looking far away out the window. Without a moment's hesitation, he offered his life for them on at least two occasions.

One time we were on Tone's farm and John was working in the field cutting grain with the binder. At four o'clock he always liked a little lunch and some cold coffee, so I packed enough for him and several of the children, and thought they could have a picnic. That would please him very much, we knew. Stella took the youngest toddler by the hand, and the basket in the other, and started across the field with two little girls straggling after. They reached the place where he was working, and were sitting peacefully eating under a tree, when a terrible rumble was heard in the distance. Looking up, they saw that Joseph's huge, fierce, horned bull was loose and was pounding across the field toward them. Telling the children to stay behind the binder and not to scare the horses, he took a pitchfork and walked slowly out into the field to meet the bull. I have told you how strong John always was, and how fearless. While the animal raced closer, John just stood still and braced himself, with the fork held steadily in his hands. The bull skidded to a stop, threw up his head, and then turned and walked away. John drove him like an old cow to his pasture and fixed the fence, while the children shook and trembled behind the binder. This bull was so fierce that he could rip up great planks in his stall, but he knew who was master on that farm.

Years later John and Emil were going through a field where a herd of cattle was grazing, when the bull broke loose and began to tear up the earth running toward them. John ordered Emil to run for the fence, while he braced himself with a club he happened to be carrying. The bull came right up, looked John in the eye, snorted and walked off.

THE THING that worried me most about our married life was that we moved and moved. John would buy one place, and would no sooner pay for it, than he would buy another. He had a weakness for gambling on property. One time for five years we worked Tone's farm, after her husband had got in poor health. For three years John ran a grocery store. He trusted everybody, and every dead-beat in town soon found it out. At last he traded the store for a farm fifty miles away in that same "Indie Land," Waupaca, where the Indians had come from to scare me as a little girl. These Indians had all moved to a reservation by that time, and the place was well settled, but I can tell you we never worked so hard in our lives getting a place in shape.

John loved every place we had so dearly that he could hardly ever be persuaded to leave it, not even to go visiting. If I wanted to go, it usually had to be with the children, and he did not like that too well. Always there was no place like home for him, and he couldn't understand why I should ever want to be away an hour. When Clara taught our home school and gave programs over there, he got a little ashamed of himself. It would not look right if the teacher's father (and treasurer of the school board) was not there. So that started him a little to going.

All throughout our fifty-five years of married life, he was the same way. If I went home to see my folks, or to visit the children, he wanted to know just what day and on what train I would be back. I would reply, "Well, John, I cannot say just now just what day I'll be back. If some of our relatives or friends ask me to come over, as they usually do, I hate to refuse them. There is no reason why you cannot stay alone for a few days, is there?"

He would answer that there was no need of visiting so much. He would be lonesome, and might get sick, too. He always hung that over my head. He never got sick, but he *might*. So I did not have much peace inside of me while I was away, thinking how he was just waiting for me to come back. He was lost the minute I was out of the house, for the first question he always asked when he came in it was, "Where's Mama?" My presence he could not live without. "Everything is wrong when you are gone, Ma," he used to say when I got back.

Poor John, he was so helpless in the house! I would find when I got back that all he had eaten while I was gone was steeped coffee. He would put the fresh coffee grounds in the coffee pot at night and drink the water in the morning. Wouldn't even boil it. All the nice things that I had fixed for him to eat before I left would be sitting there when I got back, covered with mold. All he would eat with his coffee would be some bread and butter, or raw oatmeal. No wonder he always threatened to get sick when I was gone.

I always dreaded to come back for one reason. He had a way of mussing up the house from the time he entered the door till he went out again. No matter how clean I would leave it, the floor would be knee-deep in ashes, shavings, crumbs, dirty socks, and newspapers. The first thing I always had to do was to get off my good clothes, put on old ones and start in with the broom.

KINFOLK

MY SISTERS AND brothers had just as many ups and downs as
John and I. Anguline, whose real Norwegian name was
Ingrid, was the first to marry in our family. Her husband, the
tall, full-bearded, honest, hard-working Sam Thompson, was born
and raised in Winchester right near our folks. His father, Sven, had
one of the smallest log houses around our country, but it was often
full to capacity with company. They were so hospitable to newcomers. His brother, William, was the first child born of Norwegian parents in the community, on April 17, 1848.

If Sam had been contented to stay around Winchester, we
would have been very glad. But some years before the marriage,
he and William and another brother had gone to a place about
250 miles to the northwest in Wisconsin, and had taken up home-
steads. The rich timber land was only $3.00 an acre, and you could
take up a whole section if you wanted to—640 acres. These three
brothers started something. It was not long before my brothers
John and Andrew, and sisters Anne, Hattie, and Sena had all gone
up north to these wild woods.

Imagine going to the thickest forest to start your home! What
would you do first? Anne's husband, Chris, and brother John
each took a section, but Andrew took only eighty acres. The first
thing these folks did was to clear a little place near the road for
the house and well. Then they selected good, straight, tall trees
which were hauled to the sawmill and sawed into even lengths for
house logs, and planed on one side to make a smooth interior.
Other logs were sawed into boards for floors, doors, and partitions,
if any. Anne had oak floors in her log house. After the logs were
brought back from the mill, the bark had to be peeled off with
a hand tool, and the ends hewn and shaped to fit at the corners.
The young wives worked right alongside their men, picking up
brush and burning it, taking care of the babies and animals, cooking
and washing. When enough logs were ready, the neighbors were
called in and the house put together. It was a simple beginning,
but they were all so happy and strong and thought they had discovered Eden.

Each family had a couple of cows which were allowed to roam
in the woods at will, grazing as they could. Usually at night they

181

would come home to be milked. Sometimes they got so far away that they could not find their way back, and it would not do for a person to start out in those thick woods to hunt them. If they did not return at a reasonable time the next day, someone would have to go after them. When the cows finally got back home, their udders would be nearly bursting for want of milking.

In the winter time extra men were always hired to cut wood to sell. This not only cleared the land, but it brought in a handsome profit from the wood. The wife would have a crew of men to board at $1.50 to $2.00 a week. Every bit of money helped. Some families were so poor at first that they gathered wild raspberries to sell for a few groceries.

Anguline was lucky. Sam had a log house and some farm buildings put up before he came back for his bride. They were married in the Winchester church, and our folks had a supper and dance afterward. Relatives and friends simply filled that old log house. A few days after the wedding, brother Ole took them to Medinah Junction, five or six miles away, with the horses and sleigh. Mother sorrowed afresh over this departure, for 250 miles in those days were as bad as one thousand now. Anguline did not see us again for ten or twelve years. She had three children when she came home for the first time.

She and Sam had a hard time at first in those woods. It was pioneering from the start. But they were both hard-working and saving. Sam had never had another girl, and he was very fond of his wife. Anguline had had several affairs before that, one of which was like "Speak for yourself, John." There was a certain young man very much in love with Anguline, but he was too bashful to ask for her hand. So he got a friend of his to go to her and pave the way. Now it happened that this friend was in love with our cute sister himself, and when he went on his errand, he asked her for himself. It didn't do him any good; she already had Sam on her mind.

Anguline was known always for her true character. She loved her husband and children and gave her entire life to their care. She was neat and clean, but had no system to her housework. After her daughter, Minnie, got old enough to take over, Anguline was out all day long raising chickens, calves, ducks, and geese. They had a large flock of sheep, and when it came lambing time, Anguline just about lived in the barn.

Anguline and Sam made money on every hand. They had a big maple grove, even, that yielded hundreds of dollars in maple sugar and syrup each spring. Everything they touched turned to gold. By and by the little log house was replaced by a fine eight-room brick home, filled with new furniture, even an organ. They put up big barns and all kinds of other buildings, filled with stock and chickens by the hundreds.

Their daughter, Minnie, married a very refined man named Lomo, who was a cheese-maker from Norway. Once he took Minnie on a trip back to the Old Country, and visited some of our cousins. The older ones had all died or migrated to America, so there were not many of our folks left. Lomo was so proud of this beautiful Minnie that he nearly burst when he looked at her. She had lovely features, and beautiful brown hair and eyes like her father, and besides she was so winsome that everybody loved her. Lomo was very proud showing her off to his rich parents, and showing her his fine home with servants to wait on them at every hand.

Some time after this couple returned to Wisconsin, they found that a few of their intimate friends were all excited about going to Saskatchewan, Canada, to take up a homestead. It was new land, and one could have enormous tracts of it for very little, because the government was anxious to have settlers. Lomo and Minnie decided to go with them.

I have told you how Anguline loved her husband and children. Although she was now sixty-five years old, and had every luxury her heart desired, she announced that she was going along. She said she could not live apart from that only daughter. So she and Sam sold their fine home and went. They bought enough land in Canada for themselves and their two boys. The youngest, Bennie, went with them, but the oldest, Sam, stayed in Wisconsin with his family.

I know that Anguline was never very happy out there. She and Sam were altogether too old to start another pioneer life, but they counted hardship as nothing to be near that beloved girl. The place they settled in had once been a lake, and the sod was so tough that it broke the whiffletrees. They had to get a power tractor to break the land, but when they did, the soil was so rich that they raised thousands and thousands of bushels of wheat each year. After Sam died, Anguline took a last trip home. That was when she told my children that all of them together up there, that is, her family, were worth around a million dollars.

Despite all this money, we thought it wrong for Anguline to leave her lovely home and old friends and church, and follow her children to a new country. They could have come to see her every winter. I don't believe in following your children around. When they get married, they belong to their mates, and you have to give them up. But Anguline had lots of spunk and grit, and usually got what she wanted. She was much after wealth, and she got it, more than anybody in the family. On this last trip home, she went to visit her son, Sam, in Baldwin, Wisconsin, so that she could be near a doctor. It was too far away from one in Canada. She had contracted palsy up there, and was broken down in health.

The doctors here could not help her, and she was soon bedridden. They expected her to die any time, so Minnie was sent for. Lomo, at that time, had the flu, but they did not think it very serious. He urged Minnie to go to her mother, and promised to follow just as soon as he got better. Minnie had not been in Baldwin very long when she got word that Lomo was dead. She had to go back right away to bury him and then return grief-stricken to her mother. Anguline lingered a few weeks more, and then Minnie had to take her body back to Saskatchewan to be buried beside Sam. We often said among ourselves, that for all that Anguline loved money, she could not take any of it with her when she died.

MY BROTHER Ole had a wonderful personality. He was good-looking, rather aristocratic, tall and straight and dignified. He never forgot that he was the eldest son of a rich man in Norway, and always carried himself with that air. Nobody loved fun more than he, or the good things of life, and somehow he managed to make a comfortable living without working too hard. The girls were crazy about him, and he flirted around a little when he was young, but he must have been a bachelor at heart. He used to say, "I don't need a housekeeper. I have Mother." And he never married. The folks turned the farm over to him when he became twenty-one. This was hard on him, for then he had the brunt of everything, and it was only seven years after they had come to America. But Father was nearly sixty years old then, and people were considered really old by that time. By seventy, they were just aged, and completely retired from life. That makes me laugh. Here I am eighty-three, and can travel all over the country by myself, in Pullman cars or coaches, or in automobiles with my folks. I am just as young in my mind as I was fifty years ago.

Four years ago Ole died, lacking ten days of being ninety-five. He had been living with our sister, Anne, in Rice Lake, Wisconsin, for many years, but as she had died one month before, I nursed him for four weeks through his last illness. Ole was a very devout Christian and longed to go to Heaven. His favorite hymn began like this:

> Oh, that I were in my Heavenly Home
> Away from these earthly hovels ....

He was feeble that last year he lived, but kept taking little walks every day. Up to that last year, he walked every good day up town, several blocks, where he and his cronies sat on a low window sill on the bank corner and watched the traffic, and visited. He took a cold a month before he died, and it set into pneumonia. I made every good dish that he used to like to give him strength, including *römmegröt*, but all he wanted to eat was a doughnut for breakfast, and a little coffee. Even though he had a beautiful cemetery lot in Winchester with room for eight people and only three on it, he asked us before he died not to go to the expense of taking him there. When Anne died, he had asked her husband, Chris, to buy a lot for him, too. So our good old brother, whom everybody loved, is buried in Rice Lake.

THE NEXT sister was my favorite of the whole family. Her name was Signe, but of course it became Sena in this country. From my

185

earliest days I can remember looking at her and thinking that she was the prettiest thing I had ever seen. Her eyes were dark black-blue, and could be both soft and sparkling. Like Father's, her black hair was as fine as silk, and she wore it in a pug on top of her head, with curled bangs across the forehead. I loved her sweet smile, and her soft kind voice. She was always doing something nice for people. We children knew that when she came home, we would get pretty new dresses in the latest style. She sewed for the entire family, in fact.

You can imagine that this girl would have all kinds of offers of marriage. She was one of the older girls that had to go out to do housework early, and so she met a lot of people. No tales of trouble ever came back about Sena.

Now, our sister Hattie had married a man named Halvor Olson, who was in charge of a crew of men that were building the Sault Ste. Marie Railroad up in the northern part of Wisconsin. Hattie and Halvor boarded this crew, and since Hattie was having one baby after another, they needed help and sent for Sena. Hattie and Sena had always been dear friends, and going those three hundred miles up north was a great adventure.

One day Sena met a tall handsome man with dark brown hair, parted on the side and lying in deep waves above his broad forehead. He had sharp, magnetic blue eyes, a foxy smile and a beautiful shining brown moustache curled up at the ends. He was a real dude, and dressed in the most elegant clothes. Hans Everson was a heart-smasher if there ever was one, and he won Sena's heart instantly. They had a very thick love affair, but one day she heard something about him that turned her against him, and she broke it off.

This was the time that she met Otto, the man who sent me the beaded basket for answering his letter to my parents. She became engaged to him. I am sorry to say that Sena had already broken two other engagements back home, but it looked as if she really was going to marry Otto. Then one day she met Hans again, and let the other man go. It nearly broke Otto's heart, and it was at that time that she gave him my picture out of pity, and said that I was so much like her that he would be pleased, and could have me. But

I had different ideas. What did I want with an old man like that, one I'd never seen?

Now Hans could not wait for Sena to marry him. She was twenty-eight, and it was time she settled down anyway. He was then travelling about the country, selling dressgoods, and making pretty good money. So they were married. He kept Sena dressed very well, and insisted that she curl her hair every day. He had a horse and wagon and travelled around selling the goods that he kept in a couple of big trunks in the back. Sena was settled down in Hudson, Wisconsin, where Hans's brother lived, and he came home on weekends.

Anguline's farm was only about forty miles from Hudson. One day Hans drove into the yard, knocked at the door, and asked if he could sell her some dress-goods. She had no idea who he was, and being very thrifty and saving, was in no mood to let loose of money for dresses. He was not even asked in, or invited to sit down on the porch. But he insisted, "Can't I even *show* them to you?" This annoyed her, and she stuck to her refusal, no matter how many eyes he made at her. He was so full of fun, that Hans, that he nearly choked with laughter, trying to keep a straight face. When he had exhausted his sales talks, and was about to be turned away, he burst out laughing and told her who he was. You can imagine how she felt, and how he was ushered in and treated to the best there was.

After a few years Hans quit travelling and built a big hotel in Turtle Lake, Wisconsin, where a new railroad had just gone through. He was a born money-maker, always knowing when to buy and when to sell. But he found out that he wanted to go back to travelling and sold the hotel after a while. Sena was not as happy with Hans as she thought she would be. She had to live alone a great deal of the time, and he moved her from place to place. He always provided well for her, however. They had three children, two girls, and a boy who died at birth through the carelessness of a midwife. It was the custom in those days to have a picture taken of a baby in its coffin if you had no other; I never shall forget when the picture of this pretty baby came. He was unusually large and fine, dressed like an infant prince, in his little casket.

While they were living in Ironwood, Michigan, Hans came down with typhoid fever. Sena nursed him herself, although she was again pregnant. It was not long before she took the disease herself, and died, and was buried there.

The poor little girls were passed out to relatives. Anne got the baby, and Isabel and John had the older one for a while. Hans never got over the idea of getting them back. Being very fond of our folks, Hans came to see us quite often, and every time, he brought wonderful presents for everybody, dress goods, gloves, and jewelry. By this time he had not only another hotel in Ironwood, but a saloon and a big livery stable, and was still very handsome and well dressed.

On one of his visits with us, he met my husband's sister, Julia, who had been my bridesmaid. She was a plump, good-looking girl, with round red cheeks and great big blue eyes that were full of tricks. There never was a better-hearted girl in all this world, but she had been what was known as "a fright of a young one" all her life. Her mother could do nothing with her. If she sent her to town with eggs to buy groceries, Julia would come with a red-checked tablecloth and fringed napkins, or a new hat. Strong in mind and body, she was like an untamed horse, stern and full of fun by turns. She was my children's favorite aunt, because she would romp and play with them and dress them in their best clothes until everything they had would be dirty. By the time she left, they were so spoiled that I could hardly do anything with them for a month.

Hans had two problems on his hands at this time. One was the hotel, with only strangers to run it, because he had too much other business to attend to. The other problem was those two lovely little girls, parceled out with relatives. He wanted them at home. When he met the high-spirited Julia, he thought that he had met the answer to both of these problems. In confidence he came to me and asked me what I thought about his marrying her. It was a terrible strain on me to answer such a question, being that she was John's sister, and one I thought quite a little of. But, since it has always been an impossibility for me to gloss over the truth, I told him this: "Hans, you know I'm too much related to Julia to say much. But I'll tell you this: She is a very good-hearted woman, and will be good to your children. But you will find that the difference between her and Sena is like night and day." Sena had made him proud of her wherever she went; she was capable and perfect in every way. He himself was so elegant that she suited him to a "T." With Julia, it didn't matter who heard her, or where she was, she didn't give a "Hoorah" for anyone, but would say and do anything she pleased, and was sometimes not very ladylike.

The whole family trembled to hear that he married her just the same. There never was a more ill-mated couple on earth. It was like two locomotives coming head on. He got the girls home; they were then thirteen and seventeen years old. She brought them up her way instead of his, and spoiled them just as she used to spoil mine. Both she and Hans liked to see them in fine clothes, but she was not as careful about details as the particular Hans. One day the youngest girl spilled coffee on a white dress. Julia had one of her funny notions that time, and didn't want to change it, and made her wear it to school. This was the breaking point with Hans. He got so mad that he sent the girls off to an Episcopal girls' school. It was not long before he divorced Julia.

It was a joke among my children that "he settled a building on her, but it did not crush her." On the other hand, she lived very well by herself in the same town, and defied him to the teeth whenever she could. She adopted a boy, and brought him up quite nicely. Every now and then she would come visiting us with furs and hats with big plumes and fine umbrellas, and the most rustling silks, dressed in the best right down to her skin. She had a horror of being caught with poor underwear ever since she had seen a woman, dressed like a queen on the outside, who was run over by a horse. When they had to loosen some of her fine clothing, found that she had on nothing but rags inside. Julia never forgot that sight, and her underwear was as handsome as her outside clothes. It was a sight to see her peel off all those clothes from her ample figure. She would hang all her fine jewelry around my children's necks and load them with presents. All the time she was there she would not allow them to do any work, but would help me herself. "Let the kids have fun!" was her motto. Just before meals she would stuff them with candy, and pass them anything they wanted at table, usually dessert first. You can imagine how they loved her. Every so often, Hans, who could never forget us, would come on a visit, too, and we all lived in fear and trembling that some day they would meet. But it never did happen.

THE MAN THAT Hattie married was a sort of scholarly fellow. He had only a country school education, but was so smart that he educated himself by reading. In those days, if you were a good writer, then you were considered very bright, and Halvor had one of the finest hands for writing you ever saw. He was highly respected amongst the young people, and all the girls were wild over him. He, too, was an elegant dresser. Hattie was an exceedingly pretty girl, with beautiful big blue eyes, a wealth of light brown hair, fine smooth features and a cute figure. She was a grand dancer, and as happy-go-lucky, kind, and full of wit as could be, letting each day have its worry, and then forgetting it. Hattie was so open-handed that you could have anything she possessed, and welcome to it.

At first Hattie and Halvor took a homestead in Barron County next to the farms of brother John and sister Anne. But it was soon apparent that Halvor was no farmer. He had rather work at his job of town clerk and school treasurer. Hattie said finally, "Halvor is meant to sit with a pen." They sold the farm, and with their growing family of boys, finally settled in Tower, Minnesota, where they both were very happy. Halvor was by turns a policeman and a custodian in a bank. He had a fine library of his own, and every one of their five boys was smart and decent. Nearly all made good businessmen and became well to do, and they took such excellent care of their beloved parents. Herman still owns a big department store in Tower and does a great summer-resort business in that lake country. Hattie and Halvor both died years ago.

MY BROTHER John lived alone on his homestead in the woods until he had his log house and stables up. Then he met a neighbor girl whom he had known in Winchester. She was Isabel (Ingebjorg) Daalaan Johnson, daughter of Tone's brother Björn, who came over with his family in 1883. Isabel is eighty-two now, but she can remember Norway, for she was fifteen years old before they left. She tells how she used to love going up on the *seter* with her mother. They did not own this place, but rented it. There was a lake there where they fished from a boat with a pole, string, and hook. Of a morning she loved to go up in the mountain pastures with her sisters to watch the cattle graze. The girls took turns at this. One day she would watch cattle and the next she'd stay at the cabin and work at butter and cheese-making with her mother. Those who watched cattle did handwork or picked *multer* berries for the table. All had appetites for the good food up on the *seter—gröt* for forenoon lunch, two o'clock dinner of meat and potatoes, and supper of potatoes, herring, and milk.

Sometimes people from home would come to see them, and it was good to get all the news. Who was going to be married? Was she poor or rich? Isabel used to dream that she would like to be a rich bride with beautifully embroidered apron and skirt. She did not want to be a poor girl with a *törklae* (scarf) on her head. She asked the visitor if he had heard who was going to teach the school next to the church in the fall. The *klokker* again? How was the big black cat getting along at home?

By 1883, when Björn got the "American fever," steamboats had come in. Neighbors took them in wagons as far as Kongsberg, and from there they rode in style on a train to Christiania. There they stopped a day or two waiting for the steamship "Geyser" to get ready for her long trip to America—not the long trip the sailboats made; only two weeks. They did not stop at an English port or anyplace, but sailed as straight as they could go. The passengers did not carry food chests, as Thorild and Mathis had done. Food was served on the ship; that is, they called it food. It was not very tasty—mostly soup, soup, soup. The "Geyser" was a four-deck ship with many bunks. The women slept on the upper deck, the men on the deck below.

Björn took his family first to Winchester to see his sister Tone and all the other relatives. Then he settled down in Barron County, where so many of our people had gone. These people were good to my bachelor brother. He was twenty-five and Isabel eighteen when they married. She was a fine-looking girl, tall and strong.

After a few months of courtship they were married, and they prospered from the start. They had no children, but adopted a boy who became a very good son to them. They made money on the farm, and retired about twenty years ago. John and Isabel are still both living. John is eighty-nine. He is not very well, but his eyes still twinkle with fun, and he loves to tell us stories of Norway. I do not know of an old couple that has more fun than they, playing cards and Chinese checkers. John and I are so much alike in our dispositions that we enjoy each other's visits very much.

It was strange that, coming from such a large family as ours, neither Anne, John, nor Andrew had any children. I raised the biggest family of them all. Anne mourned herself to death that she could never be a mother. She had one of Hans's and Sena's girls for nine years, and both she and her husband worshipped the child and dressed her like a doll. It just crushed her when Hans married Julia and they took the girl away from her.

Anne worked like a man alongside of Chris all her life, and they, too, became independently rich. They retired about thirty years ago and finally settled down in Rice Lake, Wisconsin. Mother lived with them for three years before she died, then they took her body back to Winchester to lie beside Father. Ole made his home with them for twenty-seven years, except for two years when he was with me. He and Anne were very fond of each other. When Anne died, in 1946, he said he wanted to go, too, and died a month later.

Sister Lena had a very hard life. Besides being lame, she was always in poor health. She married a German who was a skilled carpenter and thorough in all his work, but they had many misfortunes. Their oldest baby died in infancy. Lena is widowed now, but has a nice home in Oshkosh. Her bad luck still follows her. A few years ago she broke her hip and is still confined to a wheelchair. Her greatest blessing is her good son, Alvin, who takes care of her and the home. I do not know what she would do without him.

EARLY IN THE book I told you many times how the Norwegians made and served liquor. It was the custom to think that you couldn't be sociable without offering a "treat" to people who came. If you did not, you were considered stingy and selfish. Some could take it all right, others could not. Pretty nearly every home had its drunkard, even though that person had to suffer disgrace for his habit.

It had been said that if ten people are drinking in a room, one of them will turn out to be a drunkard. So it was at our house. There were ten of us. We all drank Mother's malt beer, and the grown-ups drank the wine she made. But one of our family very early began to show signs of weakness. It was Andres, who called himself Andrew. My John in his youth used to be in the same wild crowd, and he often told me that there was no reason to the way Andrew drank. Whereas the others were satisfied to take their alcohol, water, and sugar by the glass, Andrew would tip up the jug and drink from it, and he would drink more than anyone else. With this appetite for liquor came a terrible temper in which no one could control him. This seemed so strange to us, for Andrew was the kindest of persons when sober. I remember once he sent me a lovely set of solid gold cuff-links. I cannot look at them to this day without thinking of his good ways.

When Anguline moved to Pierce County, Andrew followed and took up eighty acres of land. I do not know how much of it was cleared before he met a rich old maid and married her. It was a mistake. Money was the cause of their trouble. In those early days, before he got really started, it all had to come through her hands, and Andrew was too high-tempered to stand the arguments that went with it. One day, when he was about forty years old, he came running out of breath to Anguline's house and said a mob was after him. She saw at once that something was wrong, and tried to nurse him, but he got only worse. Some of the near-by family had to come, and they agreed with her that he would have to be confined. They took him to the insane asylum, where he stayed until his death about twenty-five years later.

Without his liquor at the asylum, Andrew got along very well. He was made manager of the big barn, and held that job with credit all his life. Nobody could look after stock as he. He acted so sane, and like his old sweet self when the family came to visit him, and begged us so hard to get him out, that it was finally taken up with the superintendent. He replied: "Andrew is all right until he gets one of those temper spells, then you could not handle him."

Our dear mother had many sorrows in her life, the leaving of Norway, the loss of Kristine, Lena's lameness, but this one about Andrew, coming in her seventies, was worse than all of them put together. The family could not bear to tell her for a while what had happened to Andrew, then one day Father said, "Thorild, I have something on my heart that I cannot keep any longer." And he told her. If she had ever dreamed that the "treats" she dispensed with such a free and loving hand all her life, would have as their end the insanity of one of her children, she would gladly have served them a glass of cold water, or given up every friend she had. She never saw Andrew again, and it left a sore in her heart that never healed.

WAUPACA

JOHN'S AND MY last big move was to the farm in Waupaca in 1911. It was seven miles from the city, and three miles from the Wisconsin Veterans' Home, where there were many "boys in blue" still hobbling around with their canes.

John and Emil had gone ahead of us to unpack the household goods before we got there. My husband would not tell us what the place was like, but would only say, "Oh, Ma, it's wonderful!"

It was in April when he came to get us at the depot, and drove us out to the new farm. The countryside was really beautiful, all fresh and green, with cowslips in the little marshes beside the road, and birds swooping across our path. We drove for a long time enjoying the pure dry air that Waupaca is noted for. After a while we came around one of the numerous bends in the road, and John pointed to a hill in the distance. On it was a group of buildings peeking through the tall green trees, a yellow farmhouse, a big barn, some other small ones, and two beautiful blue lakes at the bottom of the hill. It was really a lovely picture, and John's eyes sparkled when he told us that that was our new home.

But when we climbed that hill and got up in the yard, we knew why he hadn't wanted us to see the place before. First of all, the yard was strewn with more junk than I had ever seen in my life— old harnesses, bottles, cans, and broken machinery. And then the house! All our lives we had lived in nice houses. This one was big enough, a tall, square, eight-room house, but its yellow paint was peeling, and the next thing I saw was that one window had the whole lower pane out. There were rags sticking in broken places in the windows upstairs, and when I went to investigate the bedrooms up there, I found a heap of rotten pumpkins and squash. The whole house was littered with rags and paper and broken plaster, and smelled ripely of mice. My furniture looked like junk in these surroundings.

John was anxious that we be pleased with our new home, but for once I almost broke down. He kept calling to us to see the lakes, and the big trees, and to look at the view across the fields and down the hill, where there was a winding river. All I could see was that we had bought a dump, and I was stuck here for better, for worse. If it had not been for our sweet daughter, Stella,

197

who was eighteen, and had quit her job and come with us for a while, I do not believe that I could have endured it. But nothing ever sat very hard on Stella, and before I knew it she was shoving things around, and clearing off the dirt and getting a fire started in the malleable iron range, and pretty soon she had me feeling better.

Stella had lovely ideas of style, and the next day we went to work to fix the place up. The grocery store had been taken in part trade for the farm, but we were still $3,500 in debt for it. What little cash John had saved, after our debts were paid in Oshkosh, had to go for horses and the wagon, and the freight bill to move our goods. Therefore we were practically stone broke, just when we could easily have used a thousand dollars on the house and barn. After twenty-five years of hard work and saving, it looked to me as if we were just back where we started.

But you can't stay blue long when you have a flock of happy children around. The three little ones were thrilled with the farm. They roamed over the fields and picked flowers to decorate the house, waded in the brooks, fished off a big stone down by the lake, climbed the trees and enjoyed themselves thoroughly. Of course, we had to put them to work, too. They were assigned the task of picking up the trash in the yard. We wondered where we were going to put it, but John solved the problem. To my amazement, he threw it in the lake, and it sank out of sight in shallow water right near shore. That was when I learned that these Waupaca lakes had no bottom. What we thought was a sandy shore, was marl and quicksand, and I forbade the children to go near it again. Emil was the only one who could swim, and he would get a rowboat and row out into the lake and go swimming after a while.

Both Emil and Stella worked like beavers that spring. Emil helped John fix up what old machinery they could find, a plow and a drag, so that they could get in the crops. The horses John had bought were some of the prettiest I had ever seen. Molly was a young mare, brown and sleek, but John did not think to try her out before buying. One of her hind legs had a spavin on it, which didn't seem to hurt her any. But when she was hitched up the first time with the other old horse, Charlie, she stood stock still. John tried every word he knew, but she would not move. We found out later that when she was hitched singly to a buggy, for instance, that she would run like a race horse. She was good for single cultivating, too, but she wanted nothing to do with a mate. So John had to get another horse to go with Charlie. Queen was her name, and we all said she certainly looked like one, so plump and pretty and full of pep. She could run like a young colt. But after we had had her a few days, she began to droop, and her hide began to hang on her bones. It was then that we knew that she had been puffed up with "condition powder." She turned out to be no good, and John had to kill her after a little while.

The mate that Charlie got finally was a spry young mare of a beautiful reddish dark brown color, a light thick mane and tail, a star on her face, and four white dainty feet. She was really a beauty, and not that alone, but you couldn't hurt her with work or on the road. No matter how tired she was, she was always lively. That horse could run in one steady trot the seven miles from Waupaca, and nobody could stop her. But beauty is as beauty does. For all her pretty face and dainty feet, she was as ugly as a devil itself. When you hitched her up, she would lift her lips and snarl, and do her best to bite your arm. When you came into the barn, she would not give a glad whinny like all our other horses, but a mad squeal, with tail switching around and around, ears back, and murderous heels kicking out behind. The only one who dared to go behind her was John, and both man and beast knew that he was not afraid of anything.

Inside the house, Stella and I were busy kalsomining and painting what we could do. The men did the rest. It was necessary to scrub all the woodwork and floors before we painted them, and quite a little plastering had to be done before we redecorated the walls. We had to cover every inch of the house with paint or kalsomine before we could get rid of the dirty smell. The cellar had to be cleaned out and new shelves put up for preserves, for the people who had last lived there had burned them for fuel. There was no place to put the butter, or anything. I had brought a couple of barrels of canned goods that I had put up the summer before.

By and by the neighbors began to be curious about what was

going on, and little by little they came. They were astonished at the change. They told us that the former owner had had twelve children, and was a morphine fiend. He was in bed most of the time and had let the place run down for years. The woman was just beaten down by child-bearing and despair. The neighbors said they had not seen the place look so nice for at least twenty years.

The second year we lived there, John remodeled the barn, and made it very nice, then built a milkhouse next to it, with a well dug right under the cement floor. Now we could water the cattle summer and winter easily. He put up a chicken coop, and corncrib. Then he built on the lake bank between the house and barn, a large building that he called a "root-house." It had two upper stories, the main floor for buggies and machinery, the second with bins for grain. It was a very handy dry place to store things I didn't need. That's where my first rocker had its final resting place, all worn out. This building had a huge cement basement under it, which would hold three thousand bushels of potatoes. There was nothing small about John's plans.

In a few years he began to remodel the house, and I can tell you when it was finished, there was some talk in the neighborhood. He fixed it up so that it was the nicest for miles around, and we now felt that we had a home as nice as the ones we had left. The kitchen had a sink with a cistern pump in it, but no running water. A well was dug under the back porch, so that it was handy winter and summer. The neighbor ladies envied me my flour bin, which swung out from the cupboard. John was always a very good cabinet-maker.

One thing I loved about this house was the double south windows in the dining room, where I had ruffled white curtains. There was a scalloped wire bracket swinging between the two windows, on which I had a thriving oxalis plant with green shamrock leaves and pink flowers that hung down. In front of this window was a long bench full of red and white geraniums, Christmas cactus, dripping purple and red fuchsias, and even two lovely amaryllis. These were the windows out of which I used to look to see my children coming over the hill, and the welcome daily visit from the mailman.

He told us that we had the largest correspondence on the route. Somehow there was always a letter to go out, for I loved to write, and there would be some to receive.

But the best thing about the new house was the front porch which stretched all the way across the house, twenty-eight feet long and ten feet wide. John put twelve windows on it, all around the sides and front, and a glass in the door. There were new full-length screens at every window. We had a long table out there, with benches and chairs to accommodate twelve or fourteen people, and we ate out there all summer. John made me a tea wagon with wheels and two shelves in the bottom. When dinner was ready we loaded up the wagon in the kitchen, wheeled it across the dining room to a window that opened to the porch, and passed the food and dishes through to the table. Oh, how happy we were when the children all came home in vacation time, and that good table was surrounded by happy faces, everybody talking and laughing at once, and the best food that I could cook passed around. When the meal was over, the cart would be loaded up again, and then taken back to the kitchen. John and I had a day bed out in the other end of the porch, where we slept in the pure fresh air from early spring till late fall, and where we took naps every day.

Stella and Emil left us to go to the county agricultural school in the fall; they stayed with Tone, who had moved to Winneconne. But Clara came home and taught the home school for the next four years, and then went up to northern Wisconsin to teach. I do not know what we would have done without that dear girl helping us out with money those first hard years on the farm. John became treasurer of the school board, and held that office for eighteen years. The younger girls went off to high school at Waupaca, and were married one by one. That left only Thelma at home with us.

It was John's ambition to give every one of his girls a watch upon graduation. Stella and Clara had got theirs in more prosperous years, but I do not know how in the world we managed to get these three younger ones a watch. Every one of the children got a gold ring about this time, too. John had been working for a rich woman who had taken in jewelry on a debt. With this, she paid John's bill, and he was tickled to death to bring home that bag of fine jewelry and let us all take our pick. Nothing made him happier than to do something nice for the children.

Thelma went through all of her eight elementary grades in our home school. After she had finished high school in Waupaca, she went out to South Dakota to attend the college where Erna's husband was teaching. After a year of this, she went into nurse's training, and while there met a man whom she married. He was a very fat person, but so good-natured that he laughed until his stomach shook most of the time. He was mayor of the little town where they lived and manager of a lumber company. This town was not far from our home, so we got to see them often. We were so happy when they brought home their first little boy, and next a dimpled little girl.

Thelma never did feel well after this last child was born. She was sick most of the time and complained of hurting inside. When the baby was five months old, Thelma had a gall-bladder operation, and her appendix was taken out at the same time. We thought she would never come out of the ether, and when she did, we could see that she was failing. An acute attack of diabetes set in. She died the next morning, before we realized what was happening.

This was the worst blow John and I had ever had. We never did get over this shock. We begged Thelma's husband for the children, but he loved them too dearly, and got a housekeeper to care for them, a woman much older than himself. We were astonished to hear about a year later that he had married her. He used to bring the family home quite often, and we were delighted, not only because we loved him, but those children were Thelma right over again. The new wife soon had two children of her own. This is what caused all the trouble. When our boy was about ten years old, and the girl eight, their father suddenly died of a ruptured appendix. He had left our children $2,000 apiece, and their share of several pieces of property. The wife claimed that he had asked her on his deathbed to keep all of his children together, but she had nothing to show for it in writing. We were simply crushed by this news, because we thought it would now be very hard to keep up with the children.

One day when John and I were sitting at home mourning over it all, a stranger happened into our house. He wanted to know what was the matter, and we told him. He said, "Are the other grandparents alive?" We said they were not. He replied, "Then don't you know that you have legal right to those children?" Well, you should have seen how the load lifted off our hearts!

The very next morning we drove to the county courthouse, and applied for the guardianship of our children. The judge told us that the stepmother had already been there and had told him that her husband had asked her to keep the children together. We were forced to bring suit against her, and it took us six months to recover them. Our lawyer was the son of the Mr. Allen, for whom I had picked hops as a girl.

If the stepmother had obeyed the judge's instructions, we might not have been so lucky. It was his ruling that the children should stay with us for four weeks every year, but after that time was up, the children begged not to go back. The judge ordered them back, and we had to take them to the courthouse.

Henrietta had been the first person in this world to hold the boy in her arms, and he had been her beloved pet since birth. When they parted at the courthouse, he gave her his pocketbook and jackknife, and the watch we had given him, and declared he was coming back to her. We could not teach them to defy the law, but Henrietta did make him learn her telephone number by heart. The girl, who had spent much of her vacation with Emil and Arline, his wife, now clung to Arline. Then the child made Arline go with her into a little room and take off the pretty clothes she had given her and put on the old dress she had come to us in. Then the little thing took Arline by the hand, and going to the judge, asked him if it would be all right if Arline kept her doll. He said it would be all right. The judge was so unreasonable in all this affair, that Erna told him: "God can see what is behind all this." At this his eyes filled with tears, he took out his handkerchief and went into his private office.

This parting was one of the most mournful moments of our whole lives. The whole town was up in arms about it, and the children wept pitifully. They declared they would not stay with their stepmother, but would run away the first chance they got. The girl's eyes snapped just as Thelma's used to. John took the boy aside and begged him never to desert his sister, and he promised.

Erna and her John from Alabama, and Emil and Arline from New Jersey, were all at Etta's house in Oshkosh the next day, so blue that they could hardly eat. Suddenly the telephone rang, and it was a long distance call. Erna answered, and a man's voice asked, "Do you have a little orphaned nephew and niece?"

Erna cried, "Where are they? Where are they?"

The man said, "I guess they're yours, all right. They are here with me in my house (about twenty-five miles away). I picked them up on the road this morning."

All Erna could say through the excitement was, "Keep them there and don't tell anyone."

It is said that Erna's John and Henrietta and Arline made that twenty-five miles in about fifteen minutes. They brought back those poor dirt-stained little children, the girl clutching her red pocketbook with the thirty-five cents that we had given her. We found out the story later. Before the stepmother had put them to bed the night before they had planned the escape. The boy was to work his way out to an alley, and then make for the highway and hide and wait for his sister. This he did the next morning. But when the sister tried to follow him, their little half-sister hung on to her and wanted her to play. The poor child had to stall around, with her red pocketbook hid under a dress that was luckily much too big for her, until she could get the half-sister interested in something else. Then she made her way out to the alley and joined her brother in his hideaway. But to her dismay, she discovered that he had a playmate that he could not shake, either, so they had to fake an excuse for being on the highway, while the playmate followed them for a long way. Finally he got tired and went back, much to their relief.

As soon as he was out of sight, the boy said, "Take hold of my hand, Sister, so you can run faster." Then they began to run, until they had gone five miles. It was a terribly hot day. Pretty soon a truck came along, and the girl thumbed a ride. The driver stopped, opened the door and let them in. Their faces were at blood heat from running, and their clothes soaked with perspiration. He asked them what they were doing, and through their exhaustion, they told him the whole story, and begged him not to tell their stepmother. This man took them home to his house, and called the number the boy gave him.

When the boy was all bathed and put in his clean pajamas and clean sheets in his little bed at night, he drew the sheets up to his chin and said, "Oh, Aunt Tetta. This is so nice!" As Henrietta went out of the room, she stooped and picked up the new little socks we had put on the boy the morning before. In each heel was an enormous hole, as evidence of the long run for freedom.

Of course, we had to have another court trial. This time the judge said that the stepmother should have them for thirty days to see if she could get along with them. After the trial, she had a man waiting outside with a car, and the children had to drive off with her again. When our daughters were eating their supper at Henrietta's house that same night, the telephone rang again, and a man asked, "Do you want to know where your children are? They are at So-and-So Orphanage at Such-and-Such a city, about one hundred miles from here."

Of course, Erna and her husband, Henrietta, and Arline were up there early the next day with the doll, pocketbooks, watch, and all the nice things the children loved, as well as a luscious picnic dinner. We did not know where to turn then, for the children refused to take their things back, for fear that they would be stolen. During the picnic, the girl would not eat, and we noticed that she was trembling from head to foot. When our daughters went home, they consulted their physician, and he said he would go there and examine the child, and apply to the judge for permission to take her away from the orphanage before she became ill.

But we were not obliged to go this far. God sees an orphan's tears. When the judge heard that the stepmother had not obeyed his order to take the children home, he was furious. Even the officials of her church heard the story. It was not long before she had to sign a paper of release. When we got the children back from the orphanage, they had head lice, and the boy had athlete's foot. But

I can tell you we were joyful. The boy went to Henrietta and her husband, and the girl to Emil and Arline. It was the girl who gave us the keynote of our delight. All the way out East to her new home, she sang, "Happy Days Are Here Again."

That girl is a trained nurse now and the wife of a young physician. The boy is a graduate of West Point.

IN THE TWENTIES, some rich men from near Chicago decided to develop their heavily-wooded lake property near our farm. Somehow they learned of John's skill at building and hired him to do the work. For the first winter he logged the property. Certainly he knew how to do that from his early days. By spring he knew every single crook and cranny of the land around six lakes and a little creek. One by one lots were sold around these shores, and John and his crews of men did all the building.

John could have made a great deal of money in this and other deals throughout his life, but he was so scrupulously honest, just like his father, Hans. He never gave anybody a chance even to suspect that he was crooked, and would take a loss many a time if he had figured short, so that his spoken word was as good as his bond. He could go to the bank at any time and get all the money he wanted without a single signer or bond.

From the very first he taught the children the same way. If they were leaving to go some where, he would ask them if they had any money. Maybe he could give them only fifty cents, but he would say, "Don't go borrowing and owing money, so that you'll lose your good name." When they went out to be married, he would say, "Live so that you will not be afraid of the knock on the door."

John was very proud of this building business. He would take us over to the places he was putting up, heft his two hundred pounds on the floor and say, "The houses I build don't shake." Very few people found fault with the quality of his work, and if anyone should dare to, he would certainly put them in their place, because he was extremely particular of its worth. Since the neighboring farmers were glad to pick up a few dollars in their odd times, he could always get a crew. Even when he was in his sixties, he still got up at five o'clock, did his chores, and was on the job by seven. He did not get to bed until nine in the evening. When there was any farm work to be done, he would hire a crew and get it done in a hurry. At other times, he would have Alec Parkhurst, the Indian, do the work. Sometimes, when he was going to be very late, I would have to do the milking. We always kept at least seven cows, and it was hard. If I was tired, I could have wished that it would be for me as it was for a certain farmer in a joke. He was so worn out that when he went to the barn, the cow said: "You're feeling so bad tonight, you just hang on, and I'll jump up and down."

Before the Chicago resorters got settled in their new summer homes, our house was headquarters for them. I often had to board them, and sold them the garden stuff and dairy products and even bread, when they began housekeeping. One of the families had three children who thought it great fun to stay on our farm. They were with us two summers. To this day I correspond with the oldest girl, Betty Castle Muirhead. She is married now, and I am sure there are few farms like hers and Bob's. He ships his pedigreed oats all over Wisconsin. After selling carloads and truck loads, he still had 16,000 bushels to sell one year. They had 3,500 bushels of soy beans, besides. As old as I am, and as young as she is, we are still the best of friends and love to hear from each other.

There was one fine piece of property left after the rush of buying was over. It was about four acres of heavily covered pine and oak woods, sloping down to Lake Menomin, the only lake that had retained its Indian name. We had some money saved up by this time, and according to pattern, John could not stand prosperity. He took the money that we had earned during those good times and built us the finest cottage of them all. Although we were now all alone, John could not think of building a house less than eight rooms. The ceiling was of polished tamarack logs. The interior walls and floor and woodwork were of the finest pine that money could buy. It was insulated with balsam wool. There were wood-burning stoves in the dining and living rooms, and an oil-range in the back kitchen. We could sleep fifteen in that place and often did, when the children all came home.

The cottage had running water from an electric pump over the well. This well was situated in a little cellar with cemented walls and floor, and so deep that it would never freeze—nine feet. It was so cold even in midsummer that we could hardly cut the butter we kept down there. There was a trap door and steps leading to this place. But for handy every-day use, he had a screened-in dumb-waiter that went on pulleys to take our victuals to the cellar. How proud John was to go out that back kitchen and demonstrate that device that he had rigged up himself!

Every time some of our friends came who had not seen the place, he could not refrain from turning on the faucets in the fine kitchen sink, so that the electric pump in the cellar would begin to throb, filling up the tank. In this kitchen I had another of his famous swinging flour bins and a handmade pastry table that folded up against the wall when not in use. There were electric lights not only in every room but in two old-fashioned square lamps that sat on high posts leading up to the garage. There were handmade bird houses everywhere, trellises for vines, cement sidewalks, and a huge sign with cement letters on the lawn up by the road, spelling "Waving Pines." We asked him where he had got that name, and he replied that in his logging days on the river, they had sung a song that went:

> The winter winds shall ne'er grow cold
> Among the waving pines.

On a summer evening how my children and grandchildren used to love to sit on that great glassed-in front porch that faced the lake, and watch the fireflies flitting over the water. We had an old high phonograph out there that I thought they would play to pieces. I never hear "Three O'Clock in the Morning" and "The Secret" without thinking of the cottage.

I slept better at this place than I had anywhere else since I was a child. A pine tree peeped in every window, that sweet scent floated through our rooms, and the soft soughing of the branches was like a lullaby. In daytime I would take my naps in a glider in a shaded nook on the lawn. John used to laugh and say that I took a dozen magazines out with me, and would go to sleep on the first one.

Henrietta and Tom and their little girl used to come to see us almost every weekend, for they lived only fifty miles away. One time, at the first, just as we were digging the cesspool, we heard a terrible yelping out there at night. John was too old to go prowling out in the woods in the dark, so we waited until morning to see what it was. Then we found that a brindle bulldog had fallen into the pit. Tom and Henrietta drove up just about that time, and Tom got a ladder and went down after the dog, coming up with it over his shoulder. The poor thing had jumped until he had nearly torn one of his toenails off. After this, Buddy was Tom's slave. Every time he heard their car coming, he would go crazy, and run up that cement sidewalk with his belly to the ground, and nearly eat Tom up.

Of course, we knew that such a beautiful animal must belong to someone, but we could never find out who. One day a man came along who said he was the dog's master, and we could tell that he was. But Buddy would not have anything to do with him. At last the man said: "I have paid out so many rewards for this dog, that if you will give him a good home, you can have him." This suited us and the dog just fine, and he was our dear pet for many years. We found out later why Buddy did not like his former master. Someone told us that they kept on pestering him to teach him tricks.

This was the happiest home John and I ever had, even though we had to live alone most of the time. One of the children had given us a radio, and that whiled away many a lonesome hour when they were not there. In the morning, the first thing John would do was to light his pipe, even before he got his shoes on. Then he would build a fire, and while he was watching it get started, he would rock and sing softly, "Guide me, O Thou Great Jehovah", and "Sweet By and By." They were his favorite hymns.

John was over seventy years old now, and he felt that he could not farm any more. He thought this thriving building business would be all he could tend to from now on, so we moved all our furniture and belongings to the cottage and rented the farm. But misfortune came. The depression began and many of the rich people lost their fortunes. John had the contract all made (but not signed) for a very fine cottage, when the woman wrote and said that she had lost every cent she had. The building business stopped right short. Along with the depression came several years of drought, and the farm didn't bring in anything. We had to move back to the farm after three blissful years, and rented the cottage instead. But that did not work so well, either. Very few people wanted so fine and big a place for their vacations. During the depression, vacationers wanted to rough it as cheaply as they could.

John had an occasional job, of course, like the time when a man came and asked him to build a wall in the bend of the creek that was washing away his land. The man wanted a pretty wall and a good wall, and he said only John could be trusted with it. John was then about seventy-two, and protested that he was too old to do that kind of work. The man said, "All you have to do is watch. You just see that the men do it right."

So John took the job, even though the depression wages were about half what they normally were. He set the men to work and tried to show them from the bank how to do it right. But he got so disgusted at their poor attempts, that he jumped into that ice-cold creek and worked there for a week, wet to his waist line. I trembled when he would come home at night, dripping from standing in that water all day long. I felt that he would be terribly sick, but I didn't realize just how strong my husband was. He didn't even take a cold. And he was always proud of that handsome wall, and never failed to point out the site as we passed on the road.

It was about this time that John took to carving. For fifty years he had kept in his mind that wonderful wooden chain he had seen in the captain's cabin while he worked on the river. Now he occupied his restless fingers with making chains and anchors and pilot wheels, bird houses, sewing boxes, lap boards, doll houses, log playhouses for the grandchildren, tea-carts, stools, and last of all nine handmade oak beds. Every one of his children and I had to have one of everything he made.

He thought about the beds a long time before he made them, for he couldn't quite get it into his mind how he wanted it to go. One day he was lying down reading the funny papers, which he enjoyed just like a child, when he gave a shout and yelled, "Here's my bed!" He showed us a picture of a bedroom in "Maggie and Jiggs." The bed had four square posts, and the head and foot were each of two long boards with small square spindles in between.

John made our beds of solid oak, and there was not a nail in them, nor did a piece of machinery touch them, except what was done at the sawmill. They were all handmade, even to the ploughing of the troughs for those small spindles. He glued little square blocks in between the spindles, both top and bottom, to hold them in place. The ends of the foot- and headboards were cut down to narrow pieces that fitted through a slot in the corner posts, and fastened there with square pegs. It seemed to come natural to John to make anything with wood that he wanted to. When he was making something, he always had some dear one in mind, and loved every minute he spent on it. "Let anybody else sleep in their fancy beds," he would say, "but I want my kids to sleep in the beds I made for them." I was the one who got the worst of it. Every winter I had to give him my kitchen, as a carpenter shop, and waded in shavings from October till May.

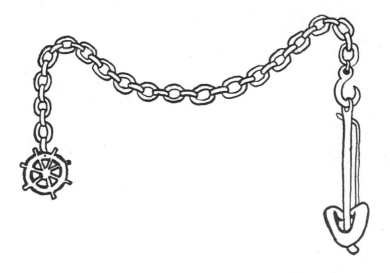

GOLDEN
WEDDING

IN THE SUMMER of 1935, when the children came home, they began to talk about our golden wedding. It was right in the middle of the depression and drought, and we wondered if any such kind of celebration would be successful, since all our relatives and old friends lived fifty miles away, and our children were scattered all over. But they would not listen to anything but that we must rejoice on that wonderful day. Unbeknownst to us, all that winter they kept writing to each other and planning the program, gifts, invitations, and everything to make the day a success.

Our fiftieth anniversary was on May 26, 1936, but that was on a Tuesday. We felt that because lots of our relatives were farmers, Sunday would be a better day, so we planned it for the twenty-fourth. The members of the Winchester Lutheran church wanted us to have it there, because John had done so much work on the church when it was built, and we had given one of the big windows. But the children preferred to have it at our old home.

We had such a lovely front lawn at the farm. John had made a big round cement table, a cement bird bath, and cement barbecue pit years before, and we had seats out there and a little log cabin where the children loved to play house. On summer days we used to go there to roast corn and weiners, and it was a nice picnic spot, under all those big oak trees.

All that spring John and I worked very hard grooming the place for the big day. The house had a cleaning such as it had not had since we first moved there. It had been newly decorated a year or so before, but I made new curtains for the dining room and kitchen. A kind Scotch neighbor, Will McCunn, helped to clean out the first floor of the root-house, which was now emptied of all machinery, because we had sold off everything. We thought that if it rained on that day we could trim it with green boughs, and the men and children could stay in there part of the time, since we expected two hundred people.

Our children began to arrive from all over the country during that week, from Alabama, New Jersey, Florida, and all over Wisconsin, bringing the little grandchildren that we loved. I can tell you that the old farmhouse was full of happy laughter again, and looked as if it would burst at the joints. John and I had laid in all sorts of supplies, and I had been baking for days before they came. Stella came home a week early and helped me. The children had brought many provisions in their cars, and mysterious packages. There was whispering in corners everywhere we looked.

Erna had furnished my wedding dress. She had asked me to send her an old dress that fitted me, and I did. This she took to a dressmaker in Birmingham, Alabama, with some beautiful delft blue rayon cloth which had white leaves and flowers in it. The buttons were small crystal balls and the collar and fichu were of white georgette and lace. The woman who made it was Mrs. Henry Bragg, grandmother of the famous football star, Harry Gilmer, who was just a young boy at the time.

BETWEEN TEN and eleven o'clock of the great day, we began to see a stream of cars coming around the bend in the road at the bottom of the hill in the distance. John had appointed Will McCunn to be traffic manager, and he took his post seriously. He was all dressed up in his best clothes, and I can still see his long arms waving the cars into orderly rows by the barn and back yard.

If ever a day had been picked out, if all the sweet breezes and blue skies and warm sunbeams had been saved for fifty years, the day of our golden wedding could not have been finer. The grass was like a thick green carpet under our feet, the trees full of new leaves, the red, yellow, and pink tulips, purple lilacs, and white spirea were blooming. All the birds had come back north and were singing and skimming around in the air above our heads. We always had so many birds around our farmhouse that they even built under the cornices, and once even on a front porch post, so that we could not use that door for weeks.

There was a big circular open space near the round cement table under the trees, where we arranged seats and benches and chairs, and planks on boxes for the people to sit on. Over to one side by the log playhouse stood a big reed organ that we had borrowed from a near-by church. We carried out several other large tables to set food on. With all these preparations, we were ready for the company when it came.

Pretty nearly all of those invited came; at least there were two hundred guests, and then we discovered afterward that we had forgotten some very dear ones, whom we had not seen for a while. It made us feel so bad. But I can tell you it was wonderful for us to see the old friends that did come, and everyone came with gifts and loaded baskets of food. We ourselves served a lot of dishes, but especially coffee and dessert. John had wanted to buy an ox and barbecue it, but I told him it was foolish to play like we had that much money during the depression. For years our relatives from Winchester had been coming in droves to our yearly picnics, and I told him we would do the same this year, only make it a little nicer.

All the old Winchester friends came: Sena and her daughters and their families, Julia (Gurina), Sarah and Eddie Uvaas and their family. Eddie was so poorly that he was sick for days afterwards, but he couldn't miss his old friends' golden wedding. Henry Larsen and his wife came, with Henry's invalid daughter, who had to be lifted out of the car. Two of Halvor and Anne Johnson's boys came with their families; one of them lived 250 miles away in northern Wisconsin. Uncle Ole Böe's son, Henry, and his wife Olga, and their family came, sons, daughters, wives and husbands, and grandchildren; cousin John Anderson and family; old neighbors like Peder Lund's stepdaughter, Anne Lund Mathison, and her husband, Morris, although Anne had such bad heart trouble that she could not speak for four days afterwards. It would take several pages to name them all, and you can imagine the glad hand-clasps and the laughter and even tears of joy as we met. Even Betsey Barstad was there, the wife of the best man at our wedding, with her household. Every person had a sweet memory behind him. Many of our folks had been friends in Norway.

All my living brothers and sisters came except Lena, who could not because of sickness in the family: brother John and Isabel, and brother Ole, Sister Anne and Chris Thompson. Anne and Chris had celebrated their golden wedding some years before, and John and Isabel were to have theirs in the fall. We thought it a remarkable thing to have a picture made of us three old couples of the same family, who had lived together fifty years, with a healthy brother Ole of eighty-eight years standing beside us.

Herman, sister Hattie's boy, came from Tower, Minnesota. His daughter, Harriet, who was attending the Moody Bible Institute in Chicago and was majoring in pipe organ, was our organist for the day.

Thelma's widowed husband came with the children, and they had such fun with all their other cousins. We have such sweet pictures of them playing in and out of the log playhouse. The husband told me later that he could hardly keep from crying all that day. When he heard Erna and Henrietta talking and laughing, it reminded him so much of Thelma that he could hardly stand it.

We had lived by this time twenty-five years in Waupaca and had numerous friends there. They all came. One of them, Laura Hartman, who had a bakery, insisted on furnishing the wedding cake. It was so big that everybody there got a nice piece. We had quite a discussion as to who could be trusted to cut that cake right, and everybody decided on Sena's daughter, Alice, who always did everything so well.

There was another group, our resort friends from Chicago, and other places. One of them, Mrs. Evenson, who with her husband had been our friend for years, was our chief soloist. Mr. Teporten, State Supervisor of Manual Training Schools in Wisconsin, gave one of the toasts. My old friend, Mrs. Castle, with whose husband John had logged the lake property years before, came from Genoa City, Illinois, with her daughter's family. I wish I could mention them all.

By the time everybody had gathered, it was time to eat. The gallon coffee pots were steaming on the malleable iron range and oil stove. There was a steady stream of people walking in and out with pitchers of cream and bowls of sugar, and baskets and boxes and crocks and jars and thermos jugs, all being set on the tables out in the yard. During this bustle, one of my daughters happened to come through the kitchen. She saw all the old Norwegian friends gathered in a ring about the cupboard, chattering in the mother tongue, and oh-ing and ah-ing and smacking their lips over something, and nodding their heads to one another. When she got up to them, one of them turned and said, "Have you tasted this good *cheese?*" Then she found that Ole Thompson, Stella's husband, had brought a large brick of a new kind of cheese from Rice Lake, and these old Norwegians, who had been brought up on so many kinds of cheese, were having a feast.

There was one thing lacking at this celebration, which nobody missed. In all the old parties, liquor had been the main "treat." I am glad to say that it had gone all out of style in our circles. Ice cream seemed to have taken its place. Nobody would think of having a party without it, and my John had bought many gallons, enough to feed the whole crowd all they could eat.

Believe me, everybody could still cook. Such lovely potato salads, and Hilda would make it different from Esther, and Lillian different from that, and we must taste them all. There were baked beans, scalloped potatoes, baked hams, fried chickens, fluffy rolls, delicious pickles and jams, bowls of bright colored jello, cakes of every size, shape, and description, doughnuts, and cookies. Myrtle would be pouring lemonade and laughing; Olga's kind face would be bent over the children, seeing that they were fed. Children didn't wait for second table any more. If there was anybody that could eat another mouthful after that dinner was over, I don't know who that could be.

"Snap-Shot Hank" Estberg had come by this time from Waupaca, and we saw to it that he had a good meal. He knew his crowds. As soon as they were stuffed into a stupor, he got them lined up on the lawn, some standing and some sitting. After our bones ached from long posing, he snapped some very good pictures of the crowd. It was a lot of work to get everyone in the crowd visible, and even then Stella's little girl showed up behind a small bush when the picture was developed, and several little boys had their heads turned to the back. Now Herman and John Xan, Erna's husband, got a police whistle, and directed the crowd to seats by the organ, while Hank took pictures of John and me.

John and I knew that there was to be a program, but it was a complete surprise as to what it would be. As I told you, the girls had been writing back and forth all year, making it up. John Xan was the master of ceremonies. While Hank was taking our picture, we could hear Harriet playing the organ, and the restless crowd was stilled by singing, "What a Friend We Have in Jesus." My

John got so nervous at the photographer's slowness in taking these pictures of us that every picture shows him with a frown.

As soon as it was over, John Xan came smiling over to us and escorted us to a seat of honor opposite the organ. Then the real program began. He read the Ninetieth Psalm, and we still remember how appropriate the tenth verse was: "The days of our years are threescore years and ten; and if by reason of strength they be fourscore years, yet is their strength labour and sorrow; for it is soon cut off, and we fly away."

Herman, who had remembered us from infancy, paid us a very tender tribute. One thing he said I shall always remember: "If I had lived a thousand miles away, I would have come to pay honor to my dear aunt and uncle on this day." Then Mrs. Evenson, who has a very fine voice, sang two numbers: "When You and I Were Young, Maggie," and "Silver Threads among the Gold." Just as everybody was ready to cry over this, she gave an encore that made us all laugh, "No, John, No," a comic song telling how a man courted his bride.

Even though it was Sunday, we had to have a Norwegian dance, of course. Henrietta had got a portable phonograph, and we enjoyed a real Norwegian wedding dance, *"Bal i Hallingdal"* (Dance in Hallingdal). June, her daughter, had taken dancing lessons for years. She wore a Norwegian country costume, white guimpe with a black sateen skirt. The little white apron had bands of green and red and blue. You should have seen those old Norwegians, nodding their heads and patting their feet as the music sounded out clear and melodious and rhythmical. Junie stamped and clapped her hands and went 'round and 'round in that old wedding dance, her short red braids swinging merrily behind. It was more fun to watch her!

Three of Clara's and Stella's boys, who were the same size, delighted everyone now with a poem by Edgar Guest. It was called "Fifty Years." Then most all of the grandchildren grouped together and sang:

> Put on your old grey bonnet
> With the blue ribbon on it . . . .

Tears were in every eye as that old song was sung in their sweet young voices.

When Mr. Teporten gave his toast, John and I wondered who he could be talking about. It couldn't be us, doing all the nice things he said. He finished by reading, "Let me live in the house by the side of the road, and be a friend to man." I guess that's what our home had been, though, all these years. People had surely been welcome.

One of the sweetest things was the history of our lives that Erna had written. It was only a few pages long, but Harriet read it so clearly that there was not a dry eye in the audience when she finished. Right after that there was a bustle and a rustle in the door of the front porch, and everybody began to squeal and laugh and say, "Oh, oh, oh!" John's and my backs were toward the house, and we could not see what was going on, until suddenly, here came a little couple dressed just like us in our wedding picture. It was Erna's daughter, Dixie, and Emil's son, Jack. They were both four years old at the time, but Jack was slightly taller, and he was holding Dixie by the hand. Jack looked so much like John, and Dixie like me with her red hair, that everybody got the idea right away. So many in the crowd had that wedding picture in their photograph albums that everybody recognized it. Jack had on long tight black pants, with a cut-away jacket, a big loose black tie on a stiff white collar, and a white artificial flower in his buttonhole.

Dixie had on almost a duplicate of my wedding dress. Harry Gilmer's grandmother had made this, too. It was of brown satin with tucks across the front. There was a tight waist and long sleeves; the neck had white ruching around it, and there were buttons all the way to the waist. Around her neck hung the heavy gold chain with the fat blue enameled locket that John had given me as a wedding gift. Her red hair was fixed as mine used to be, with curled bangs, topped by a wreath of white artificial flowers. Jack handed John a button-hole bouquet of real flowers, and Dixie gave me a beautiful corsage of white and yellow flowers that Arline had bought. Some of our girls rushed forward to pin them on. Then Jack took Dixie by the hand again, and facing her, sang, with his baby lisp and all, in a clear voice all could hear:

When Your Hair hath turned to Thilver
I will love you just the Thame. . . .

Following this there was the presentation of the large gifts, a
generous purse of money from guests, and a chest of flat silver
from the children. The last thing on the program was a song: "Until the End of Time," sung by a Mr. Bodeen, who was Clara and
Hjalmer's old friend from Rice Lake. He had come all that 250
miles just to sing for us that day. It was worth it, for us at least.
He had a wonderfully fine voice, and the song just put the right
finish to the program.

After it was over, we all visited and talked of old times, and then
one by one the friends began to leave, at least those who lived far
away. Some of the others stayed and had coffee and lunch or
supper. Dixie, who had missed her usual nap, and was now a little
fussy, got hold of her father's police whistle and put all her aunts
and uncles and cousins through a drill, and had them pose for a
snapshot. She knew just where she wanted them to stand.

It is something to live together for half a century, raise a nice big
family of children, and have your friends and relatives rejoice with
you. I can tell you we were weary that night, but we slept with
light hearts at all the happy memories.

A FEW DAYS after that, before the children began to leave, John
and I decided that this was the time to divide the heirlooms. If that
task is left until the old folks are gone, there are often hard feelings
and trouble. We said we would do it right then. So I gathered all
my girls together around me in the parlor, by the big shirtwaist box
that Harry had made for me once, where I kept my treasures, and
we set to it. Henrietta was given a piece of paper and a pencil, and
told to write down what everyone should get. The choicest piece in
the whole chest, of course, was the heavy gold wedding chain. It
had been settled long ago that that should go to the oldest daughter,
Clara, and she was tickled about it. The other things were fingered
lovingly and distributed, and there was not a bit of quarreling about
it. Everybody agreed on the idea that we should leave these things
in the shirtwaist box, and then after we were gone, it should be done

with them as the paper said. Then the list was put among our important papers. We decided who should have the battle-ax that my father had found in the Norwegian mountains, the gold-headed carved cane that belonged to Captain Martin Oleson, the cane from Lincoln's birthplace, the wedding guimpe that had been made and worn by my grandmother, Signe, in 1810, the strips of ceremonial belt that all the grandmothers had worn for generations back. There were silver buttons from my father's coats and trousers, a silver spoon from Norway, old dishes, old books, the clock with the angel on it, the clock that my father had carried home on his back the year I was born. None of us ever regretted the decisions made on that day.

When I look at that golden wedding picture now, I sigh. Right after it was taken, certain of the old friends began to die off. Thelma's husband was among the first. Clara's husband and Tom died. Now only a few of the old relatives are left. My John is gone, and the two Waupaca homes we loved have been sold.

I am now eighty-three years old and make my home with Stella and Ole in Rice Lake, Wisconsin. They are very good to me. Every year there is some kind of visit to the scattered children. Only a few years ago I made a railway journey from Rice Lake to Tampa, Florida, to see Harry and Frances and the children. No one went with me, and it went just fine. I still make my own clothes and summer coats, and can crochet and knit almost anything. Recently I made an all-over lace and organdy evening dress for a young lady granddaughter to wear in a piano recital. They all still beg me to bake bread and cookies. I am not as strong as I was, and I now need two naps a day, one after dinner, and one at the "tailor's hour." But as long as I can get around and be useful, I shall be most grateful to God.

If I cannot go South to see my children, they come to see me. Erna's John is a college professor in Alabama. They like it down there real well. But each year when vacation time comes, they drive home for a cool rest. John began to notice that every time they crossed the Wisconsin line, Erna's eyes would fill with tears. "Why are you crying?" he would ask.

"I don't know," she would reply. "It's just so good to be home."

223

It was in the midst of the depression, but John said, "I'm going to buy you a little bit of this state, if it's the last thing I do." And that very summer, 1936, he bought a beautiful lot at Island Point on Lake Winnebago, and gave it to her as a gift. They built a little log cabin there, and invite me to spend the summers with them. We look out over the lake where the tugboats move along slowly on the other side of the island, and think of my John towing logs with his Uncle Ole's tugboat on that same route sixty-four years ago. Down the road a way is the white house that he built before Erna was born, and where we spent some happy years. A short auto ride will take us to the old log house where I first opened my eyes. We visit the old Winchester church and the graveyard where our loved ones lie, and I see friends I've known all my life.

No matter where we go, we all come back to the place where the Oleson family was established in America 107 years ago. Wisconsin is my home.

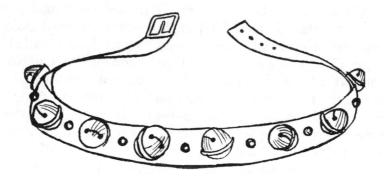

GENEALOGICAL
TABLES

IT WAS THE author's first intention to give complete genealogies of the Haevre, Böe, Skare, and Daalaan families. But when more than a thousand names had been assembled and listed, the tables became so voluminous that they far exceeded the needs of the book, and a shorter form was considered more appropriate.

In the following pages, Table I shows the forebears and the descendents of John and Thurine Oleson; Tables II, III, IV, and V show the families of each of their parents down to and including the generation to which John and Thurine belong.

An asterisk (*) following a surname indicates that it is a farm name (see above, pages 117-18); a dagger (†) indicates a member of the family who remained in Norway; a double dagger (‡) indicates a member who died in childhood.

TABLE I

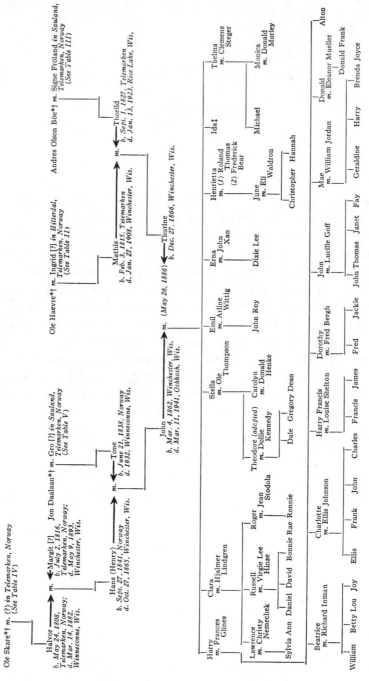

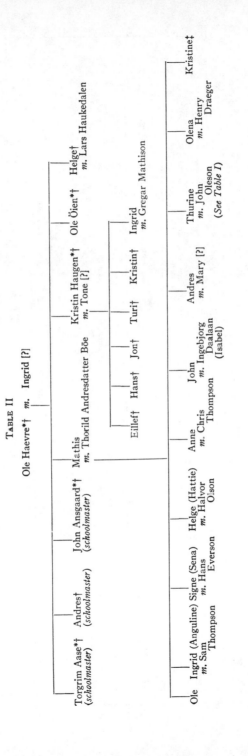

TABLE II

Ole Haevre*† *m.* Ingrid [?]

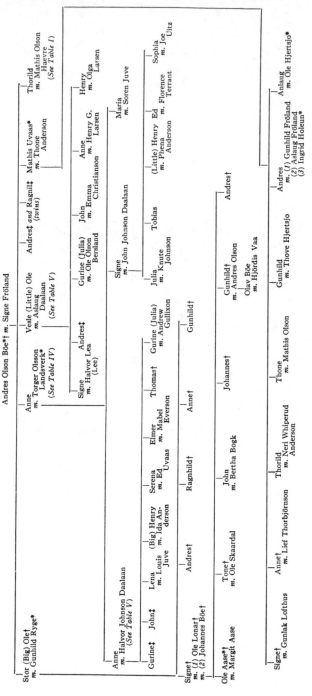

TABLE III

TABLE IV

Ole Skare*† m. [?]

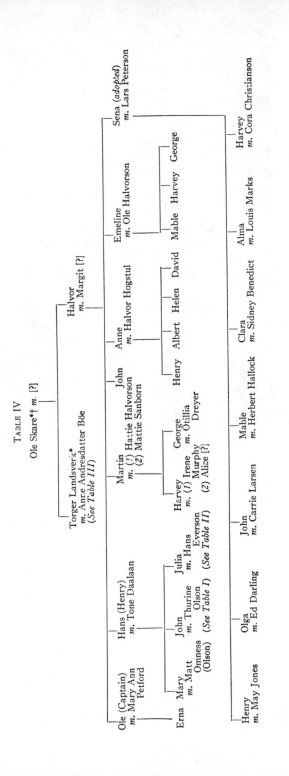

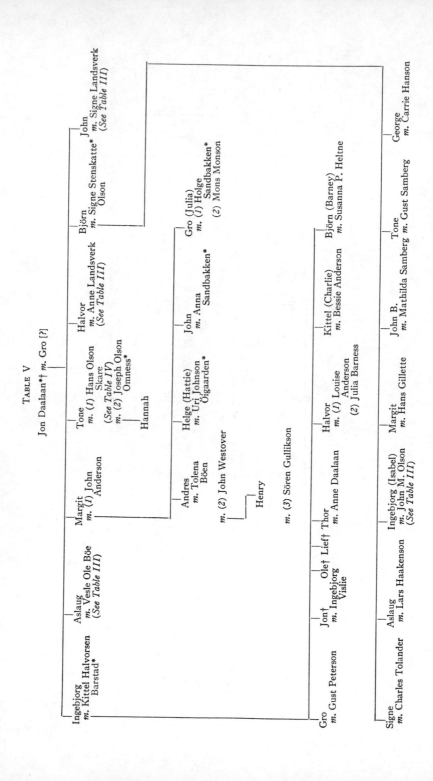

TABLE V